ONLY BELIEVE

for the

HOLY SPIRIT

ONLY BELIEVE

for the

HOLY SPIRIT

Smith
WIGGLESWORTH

WHITAKER
HOUSE

ONLY BELIEVE FOR THE HOLY SPIRIT
90 Day Devotional

This book contains edited excerpts from *Smith Wigglesworth Devotional*, © 1999 by Whitaker House.

ISBN: 979-8-88769-218-0
eBook ISBN: 979-8-88769-219-7
Printed in the United States of America

Whitaker House
1030 Hunt Valley Circle
New Kensington, PA 15068
www.whitakerhouse.com

Library of Congress Control Number: 2024937448

1 2 3 4 5 6 7 8 9 10 11 ꟺ 30 29 28 27 26 25 24

CONTENTS

SECTION ONE: BAPTISM OF THE HOLY SPIRIT

SECTION TWO: POWER OF THE HOLY SPIRIT

SECTION THREE: GIFTS OF THE HOLY SPIRIT

SECTION FOUR: LIVING IN THE HOLY SPIRIT

DAY 1

A BETTER PLAN FOR YOU

Be you faithful to death, and I will give you a crown of life.
—Revelation 2:10

Scripture reading: Acts 6:1–7; Revelation 2:9–11

The Twelve told the rest of the disciples to find seven men to look after the business side of things. They were to be men with a good reputation and filled with the Holy Spirit. Those who were chosen were just ordinary men, but they were filled with the Holy Spirit, and this infilling always lifts a man to a plane above the ordinary. He can baptize you "*with the Holy Spirit and fire*" (Matthew 3:11 NKJV).

The multitude chose seven men to serve tables. Undoubtedly, they were faithful in their appointed tasks, but we see that God soon had a better plan for two of them—Philip and Stephen. Philip was so full of the Holy Spirit that he could have a revival wherever God put him down. (See Acts 8:5–8, 26–40.) Man chose him to serve tables, but God chose him to win souls.

Oh, if I could only stir you up to see that, as you are faithful in the humblest role, God can fill you with His Spirit, make you a chosen vessel for Himself, and promote you to a place of mighty ministry in the salvation of souls and in the healing of the sick. Nothing is impossible to a man filled with the Holy Spirit. The possibilities are beyond all human comprehension. When you are filled with the power of the Holy Spirit, God will wonderfully work wherever you go.

When you are filled with the Spirit, you will know the voice of God. I want to give you one illustration of this. When I was going to Australia recently, our boat stopped at Aden and Bombay. In Aden the people came around the ship selling their wares—beautiful carpets and all sorts of Oriental things. One man was selling some ostrich feathers. As I was looking over the side of the ship watching the trading, a gentleman said to me, "Would you join me in buying that bunch of feathers?" What did I want with feathers? I had no use for such things and no room for them either. But the gentleman asked me again, "Will you join me in buying that bunch?" The Spirit of God said to me, "Do it."

The feathers were sold to us for three pounds, and the gentleman said, "I have no money on me, but if you will pay the man for them, I will send the cash down to you by the steward." I paid for the feathers and gave the gentleman his share. He was traveling first class, and I was traveling second class. I said to him, "No, please don't give that money to the steward. I want you to bring it to me personally in my cabin." I asked the Lord, "What about these feathers?" He showed me that He had a purpose in my purchasing them.

A little while later, the gentleman came to my cabin and said, "I've brought the money." I said to him, "It is not your money that I want; it is your soul that I am seeking for God." Right there he opened up the whole story of his life and began to seek God, and that morning he wept his way through to God's salvation.

You have no idea what God can do through you when you are filled with His Spirit. Every day and every hour you can have the divine leading of God. To be filled with the Holy Spirit is great in every respect.

Thought for today: It does not take a cultured or an educated man to fill a position in God's church. What God requires is a yielded, consecrated, holy life, and He can make it a flame of fire.

DAY 2

THE SWEET TOUCH OF HEAVEN

To whom coming, as to a living stone, disallowed indeed of men, but chosen of God, and precious.
—1 Peter 2:4

Scripture reading: 1 Peter 2:1–16

I know many of you think before you speak. Here is a great word: *"For your obedience is come abroad to all men. I am glad therefore on your behalf: but yet I would have you wise to that which is good, and simple concerning evil"* (Romans 16:19). Innocent. No inward corruption or defilement, that is, not full of distrust, but a holy, divine likeness of Jesus that dares believe that the almighty God will surely watch over all. Hallelujah! *"There shall no evil befall you, neither shall any plague come near your dwelling. For He shall give His angels charge over you, to keep you in all your ways"* (Psalms 91:10–11). The child of God who is rocked in the bosom of the Father has the sweetest touch of heaven, and the honey of the Word is always in his life.

If the saints only knew how precious they are in the sight of God (see Isaiah 43:4), they would scarcely be able to sleep for thinking of His watchful, loving care. Oh, He is a precious Jesus! He is a lovely Savior! He is divine in all His attitudes toward us, and He makes our hearts burn. There is nothing like it. "Oh," said the two men who had traveled to Emmaus with Jesus, *"Did not our heart burn within us, while He talked with us by the way?"* (Luke 24:32.) Oh, beloved, it must be so today.

Always keep in mind that the Holy Spirit must bring manifestation. We must understand that the Holy Spirit is breath, the Holy Spirit is a person, and it is the most marvelous thing to know that this Holy Spirit power can be in every part of our bodies. You can feel it from the crown of your head to the soles of your feet. Oh, it is lovely to be burning all over with the Holy Spirit! And when that takes place, the tongue must give forth the glory and the praise.

You must be in the place of magnifying the Lord. The Holy Spirit is the great Magnifier of Jesus, the great Illuminator of Jesus. After the Holy Spirit comes in, it is impossible to keep your tongue still. Why, you would burst if you didn't give Him utterance! What about a silent baptized soul? Such a person is not to be found in the Scriptures. You will find that when you speak to God in the new tongue He gives you, you enter into a close communion with Him never experienced before. Talk about preaching! I would like to know how it will be possible for all the people filled with the Holy Spirit to stop preaching. Even the sons and daughters must prophesy. (See Joel 2:28.) After the Holy Spirit comes in, a man is in a new order in God. You will find it so real that you will want to sing, talk, laugh, and shout. We are in a strange place when the Holy Spirit comes in. If the incoming of the Spirit is lovely, what must be the outflow? The incoming is only to be an outflow.

I am very interested in scenery. When I was in Switzerland, I wasn't satisfied until I went to the top of the mountain, though I like the valleys also. On the summit of the mountain, the sun beats on the snow and sends the water trickling down the mountain right through to the meadows. Go there and see if you can stop the water. It is the same way in the spiritual realm. God begins with the divine flow of His eternal power, which is the Holy Spirit, and you cannot stop it.

Thought for today: Faith is the open door through which the Lord comes in.

DAY 3

SPIRITUAL GIANTS

Why look you so earnestly on us, as though by our own power or holiness we had made this man to walk?
—Acts 3:12

Scripture reading: Acts 3:2–26

We must always clearly see that the baptism in the Spirit must make us ministering spirits. Peter and John had been baptized only a short time when they met the lame man at the temple. Did they know what they had? No. I challenge you to try to know what you have. No one knows what he has in the baptism in the Holy Spirit. You have no conception of it. You cannot measure it by any human standards. It is greater than any man can imagine; consequently, those two disciples had no idea what they had.

For the first time after they had been baptized in the Holy Spirit, they came down to the Gate Beautiful. There they saw the man sitting who had been lame for over forty years. What was the first thing that happened after they saw him? Ministry. What was the second? Operation. What was the third? Manifestation, of course. It could not be otherwise. You will always find that this order in the Scriptures will be carried out in everybody.

I clearly see that we ought to have spiritual giants in the earth, mighty in understanding, amazing in activity, always having a wonderful testimony because of their faith-filled works. I find instead that there are many people who perhaps have better discernment than the average believer, better knowledge of the Word than the average believer, but they have failed to put their discernment and knowledge into practice, so the gifts lie dormant. I am here to help you to begin doing mighty acts in the power of God through the gifts of the Spirit. You will find that what I am speaking about is from personal knowledge derived from wonderful experiences in many lands. The man who is filled with the Holy Spirit is always acting. The first verse of the Acts of the Apostles says, *"Jesus began both to do and teach"* (Acts 1:1). Jesus had to begin to do, and so must we.

Thought for today: I would rather have the Spirit of God on me for five minutes than receive a million dollars.

DAY 4

A DOUBLE CURE

You shall receive power when the Holy Spirit has come upon you.
—Acts 1:8 (NKJV)

Scripture reading: Romans 5:19–6:18

My friend, you need a double cure. You first need saving and cleansing and then the baptism of the Holy Spirit, until the old man never rises anymore, until you are absolutely dead to sin and alive to God by His Spirit and know that old things have passed away. When the Holy Spirit gets possession of a person, he is a new being entirely—he becomes saturated with divine power. We become a habitation of Him who is all light, all revelation, all power, and all love. Yes, God the Holy Spirit is manifested within us in such a way that it is glorious.

A certain rich man in London had a flourishing business. He used to count his many assets, but he was still troubled inside; he didn't know what to do. Walking around his large building, he came upon a boy who was the doorkeeper; he found the boy whistling. Looking at him, he sized up the whole situation completely and went back to his office again and puzzled over the matter. Although he continued with his business, he could find no peace. His bank could not help him; his money, his success, could not help him. He had an aching void. He was helpless within. My friend, having the world without having God is like being *"whited sepulchers"* (Matthew 23:27).

When he could get no rest, he exclaimed, "I will go and see what the boy is doing." Again he went and found him whistling. "I want you to come into my office," he said. When they entered the office, the man said, "Tell me, what makes you so happy and cheerful?" "Oh," replied the boy, "I used to be so miserable until I went to a little mission and heard about Jesus.

Then I was saved and filled with the Holy Spirit. I am always whistling inside; if I am not whistling, I am singing. I am just full!"

This rich man obtained the address of the mission from the boy, went to the services, and sat near the door. But the power of God moved so strongly that when the altar call was given, he responded. God saved him and, a few days afterward, filled him with the Holy Spirit. The man found himself at his desk, shouting, "Oh, hallelujah!"

The blessed Son of God wants to fill us with such glory until our whole body is aflame with the power of the Holy Spirit. I see there is *"much more"* (Romans 5:9). Glory to God! My daughter asked some African boys to tell her the difference between being saved and being filled with the Holy Spirit. "Ah," they said, "when we were saved, it was very good; but when we received the Holy Spirit, it was more so." Many of you have never received the "more so."

After the Holy Spirit comes upon you, you will have power. God will mightily move within your life; the power of the Holy Spirit will overshadow you, inwardly moving you until you know there is a divine plan different from anything that you have had in your life before.

Has He come? He is going to come to you. I am expecting that God will so manifest His presence and power that He will show you the necessity of receiving the Holy Spirit. Also, God will heal those who need healing. Everything is to be had now: salvation, sanctification, the fullness of the Holy Spirit, and healing. God is working mightily by the power of His Spirit, bringing to us a fullness of His perfect redemption until every soul may know that God has all power.

Thought for today: God is the essence of joy to us in a time when all seems barren, when it seems that nothing can help us but the light from heaven that is far brighter than the sun. When that touches you and changes you, you realize nothing is worthwhile but that.

DAY 5

BE SATISFIED

If any man thirst, let him come to Me, and drink.
—John 7:37

Scripture reading: John 7:37–8:12

Most of us have seen water baptism in action so often that we know what it means. But I want you to see that God's very great desire is for you to be covered with the baptism of the Holy Spirit. He wants you to be so immersed with the light and revelation of the Holy Spirit, the third person of the Trinity, that your whole body will be not only filled but also covered over until you walk in the presence of the power of God.

Jesus saw all the people at the Feast of Tabernacles, and He not only had a great ability to scrutinize, to unfold the inward thoughts and intents of the heart, but He also saw things at a glance; He took in a situation in just a moment's time.

We must not forget that He was filled with the Holy Spirit. He was lovely because He was full of the divine inflow of the life of God. Look at how He dealt with this situation. He saw the people who had been at Jerusalem at the feast, and they were coming back dissatisfied. My Lord could never be satisfied when anybody was dissatisfied.

Nowhere in Scripture is it recorded that you should be famished, naked, full of discord, full of evil, full of disorder, full of sensuality, or full of carnality. That was what was taking place at the feast, and they came away hungrier than they were before. Jesus saw them like that, and He said, "*Ho, every one that thirsts, come you to the waters*" (Isaiah 55:1). Come to Me, you who are thirsty, and I will give you drink.

Oh, the Master could give! The Master had it to give. Beloved, He is here to give, and I am sure He will give.

Yes, the heavy hand of God is full of mercy. The two-edged sword is full of dividing. (See Hebrews 4:12.) His quickening Spirit puts to death everything that needs to die so that He might transform you by the resurrection of His life.

Thought for today: The death of Christ brings forth the life of Christ.

DAY 6

FREEDOM FROM FEAR

There is no fear in love; but perfect love casts out fear.
—1 John 4:18

Scripture reading: 1 John 4:7–21

Never be afraid of anything. There are two things in the world: one is fear, the other faith. One belongs to the devil, the other to God. If you believe in God, there is no fear. If you sway toward any delusion of Satan, you will be brought into fear. Fear always brings bondage. There is a place of perfect love for Christ in which you are always casting out all fear and you are living in the place of freedom. (See 1 John 4:18.) Be sure that you never allow anything to make you afraid. God is for you; who can be against you? (See Romans 8:31.)

The reason why so many people have gone into Christian Science is that the church is barren; it does not have the Holy Spirit. Christian Science exists because the churches have a barren place where the Holy Spirit has not been allowed to rule. There would be no room for Christian Science if the churches were filled with the Holy Spirit, but because the churches had nothing, then the needy people went to the devil to fill the void, and he persuaded them that they had something. Now the same people are coming out knowing they have had nothing—only a wilderness experience.

Let us save ourselves from all this trouble by letting the Holy Spirit fill our hearts. Don't depend on any past tense, any past momentum, but let the anointing be upon you, let the presence and the power be upon you. Are you thirsty, longing, desiring? Then God will pour out of His treasures all you need. God wants to satisfy us with His great, abounding, holy love, imparting love upon love and faith upon faith.

If you have fallen short, it is because you refused the Holy Spirit. Let the Holy Spirit be light in you to lighten even the light that is in you, and no darkness will befall you; you will be kept in the middle of the road.

Be careful when anybody comes to you with a sugarcoated pill or a slimy tongue. The Spirit of the Lord always deals with truth. Give the devil the biggest chase of his life by saying these words: *"If we walk in the light, as He is in the light, we have fellowship one with another, and the blood of Jesus Christ His Son cleanses us from all sin"* (1 John 1:7).

Look to the coming of the Lord. Be at peace, live in peace, forgive, and learn how to forgive. Never bear malice; don't hold any grudge against anybody. Forgive everybody. It does not matter whether they forgive you or not, you must forgive them. Live in forgiveness; live in repentance; live wholeheartedly. Set your house in order, for God's Son is coming to take what is in the house.

Thought for today: The cause of all deterioration is refusal of the Holy Spirit.

DAY 7

FILLED WITH THE SPIRIT

Be not conformed to this world: but be you transformed by the renewing of your mind, that you may prove what is that good, and acceptable, and perfect, will of God.
—Romans 12:2

Scripture reading: 2 Corinthians 4

God wants to make us pillars: honorable, strong, and holy. God will move us on. I am enamored with the possibility of this. God wants you to know that you are saved, cleansed, delivered, and marching to victory. He has given you the faith to believe. God has a plan for you! "*Set your affection on things above*" (Colossians 3:2), and get into the heavenly places with Christ.

You cannot repeat the name of Jesus too often. What a privilege it is to kneel and get right into heaven the moment we pray, where the glory descends, the fire burns, faith is active, and the light dispels the darkness.

Jesus is the Light and the Life of men; no man can have this light and still walk in darkness. (See John 8:12.) "*When Christ, who is our life, shall appear, then shall you also appear with Him in glory*" (Colossians 3:4). Where His life is, disease cannot remain. Is not He who dwells in us greater than all? Is He greater? Yes, when He has full control. If one thing is permitted outside the will of God, it hinders us in our standing against the powers of Satan. We must allow the Word of God to judge us, lest we stand condemned with the world. (See 1 Corinthians 11:32.)

"*When Christ, who is our life, shall appear, then shall you also appear with Him in glory*" (Colossians 3:4). Can I have any life apart from Him, any joy or any fellowship apart from Him? Jesus said, "*The prince of this world comes, and has nothing in Me*" (John 14:30). All that is contrary in us is withered by the indwelling life of the Son of God.

Are we ready? Have we been clothed with the Holy Spirit? Has mortality been swallowed up in life? If He who is our life came, we should go. I know that the Lord laid His hand on me. He filled me with the Holy Spirit.

Heaven has begun within me. I am happy now, and free, since the Comforter has come. The Comforter is the great Revealer of the kingdom of God. He came to give us the more abundant life. God has designed the plan, and nothing else really matters because the Lord loves us. God sets great store in us.

The way into glory is through the flesh being torn away from the world and separated unto God. This freedom of spirit, freedom from the law of sin and death, is cause for rejoicing every day. The perfect law destroys the natural law. Spiritual activity takes in every passing ray, ushering in the days of heaven upon earth, when there is no sickness and when we do not even remember that we have bodies. The life of God changes us and brings us into the heavenly realm, where our reign over principalities and over all evil is limitless, powerful, and supernatural.

If the natural body decays, the Spirit renews. Spiritual power increases until, with one mind and one heart, the glory is brought down over all the earth, right on into divine life. When the whole life is filled, this is Pentecost come again. The life of the Lord will be manifested wherever we are, whether in a bus or on a train. We will be filled with the life of Jesus unto perfection, rejoicing in hope of the glory of God (see Romans 5:2), always looking for our translation into heaven.

I must have the overflowing life in the Spirit. God is not pleased with anything less. It is a disgrace to be part of an ordinary plan after we are filled with the Holy Spirit. We are to be salt in the earth (see Matthew 5:13). We are to be hot, not lukewarm (see Revelation 3:16), which means seeing God with eagerness, liberty, movement, and power. Believe! Believe!

Thought for today: The life of the Lord in us draws us as a magnet, with His life eating up all else.

DAY 8

BE MADE NEW

But what things were gain to me, those I counted loss for Christ. Yea doubtless, and I count all things but loss for the excellency of the knowledge of Christ Jesus my Lord.
—Philippians 3:7–8

Scripture reading: 2 Corinthians 5

Daily, there must be a revival touch in our hearts. God must change us after His fashion. We are to be made new all the time. There is no such thing as having all grace and knowledge. God wants us to begin with these words of power found in Philippians 3 and never stop but go on to perfection. I am positive that no man can attain like-mindedness except by the illumination of the Spirit.

God has been speaking to me over and over that I must urge people to receive the baptism of the Holy Spirit. In the baptism of the Holy Spirit, there is unlimited grace and endurance as the Spirit reveals Himself to us. The excellency of Christ can never be understood apart from illumination. I must witness about Christ. Jesus said to Thomas, *"Thomas, because you have seen Me, you have believed: blessed are they that have not seen, and yet have believed"* (John 20:29).

There is a revelation that brings us into touch with Him where we get all and see right into the fullness of Christ. As Paul saw the depths and heights of the grandeur, he longed that he might gain Him. Before his conversion, in his passion and zeal, Paul would do anything to bring Christians to death. His passion raged like a mighty lion. As he was going to Damascus, he heard the voice of Jesus saying, *"Saul, Saul, why persecute you Me?"* (Acts 9:4). What touched him was the tenderness of God.

Friends, it is always God's tenderness that reaches us. He comes to us in spite of our weakness and depravity. If somebody came to oppose us, we would stand our ground, but when He comes to forgive us, we do not know what to do. Oh, to gain Christ! A thousand things in the nucleus of a human heart need softening a thousand times a day. There are things in us that unless God shows us *"the excellency of the knowledge of Christ Jesus"* (Philippians 3:8), we will never be broken and brought to ashes. But God will do it. We will not merely be saved, but we will be saved a thousand times over! Oh, this transforming regeneration by the power of the Spirit of the living God makes me see there is a place to *"gain Christ"* (Philippians 3:8 NKJV), so that I may stand complete there. As He was, so am I to be.

We cannot depend upon our works, but upon the faithfulness of God, being able under all circumstances to be hidden in Him, covered by the almighty presence of God. The Scriptures tell us that we are in Christ and Christ is in God. (See 1 Corinthians 3:23.) What is able to move you from this place of omnipotent power? *"Shall tribulation, or distress, or persecution, or famine, or nakedness, or peril, or sword?"* (Romans 8:35). Oh no! Will life, or death, or principalities, or powers? (v. 38). No, *"we are more than conquerors through Him that loved us"* (v. 37).

Thought for today: The Holy Spirit is the great Illuminator who makes me understand all the depths of Him.

DAY 9

RECEIVE THE HOLY SPIRIT

That the blessing of Abraham might come on the Gentiles through Jesus Christ.
—Galatians 3:14

Scripture reading: John 16:7–22

When we have the right attitude, faith becomes remarkably active. But it can never be remarkably active in a dead life. When sin is out, when the body is clean, and when the life is made right, then the Holy Spirit comes, and faith brings the evidence.

Why should we tarry, or wait, for the Holy Spirit? Why should we wrestle and pray with a living faith to be made ready? Because we need the Holy Spirit to convict the world of sin, righteousness, and judgment—that is why the Holy Spirit is to come into your body. First of all, your sin is gone, and you can see clearly to speak to others. But Jesus does not want you to point out the speck in somebody else's eye while the plank is in your own. (See Matthew 7:3–5.)

The place of being filled with the Holy Spirit is the only place of operation where the believer binds the power of Satan. Satan thinks that he has a right, and he will have a short time to exhibit that right as the Prince of the World, but he can't be prince as long as there is one person filled with the Holy Spirit. That is why the church will go before the tribulation.

Now, how do you dare resist coming into the place of being filled with the life and power of the Holy Spirit? What is the attitude of your life? Are you thirsty? Are you longing? Are you willing to pay the price? Are you willing to forfeit in order to have? Are you willing to allow yourself to die so that He may live? Are you willing for Him to have the right-of-way in your heart, your conscience, and all you are? Are you ready to have God's deluge of blessing upon your soul? Are you ready to be changed forever, to receive the Holy Spirit, to be filled with divine power forever?

Thought for today: There are two sides to the baptism of the Holy Spirit: the first condition is that you possess the baptism; the second is that the baptism possesses you.

DAY 10

ASK IN FAITH

Ask, and it shall be given you; seek, and you shall find; knock, and it shall be opened to you.
—Matthew 7:7

Scripture reading: Hebrews 11

Many people do not receive the Holy Spirit because they are continually asking and never believing. *"Every one that asks receives"* (Matthew 7:8). He who is asking is receiving; he who is seeking is finding. The door is being opened right now; that is God's present Word. The Bible does not say, "Ask and you will not receive." Believe that asking is receiving, seeking is finding, and to him who is knocking, the door is being opened.

When will we see people filled with the Holy Spirit and things done as they were in the Acts of the Apostles? It will be when people say, "Lord, You are God." I want you to come into a place of such relationship with God that you will know your prayers are answered because He has promised.

Faith has its request. Faith claims it because it has it. *"Faith is the substance of things hoped for"* (Hebrews 11:1). As sure as you have faith, God will give you the overflowing, and when He comes in, you will speak as the Spirit gives utterance. (See Acts 2:4.)

You must come to a place of ashes, a place of helplessness, a place of wholehearted surrender where you do not refer to yourself. You have no justification of your own in regard to anything. You are prepared to be slandered, to be despised by everybody. But because of His personality in you, He reserves you for Himself because you are godly, and He sets you on high because you have known His name. (See Psalm 91:14.) He causes you to be the fruit of His loins and to bring forth His glory so that you will no longer rest in yourself. Your confidence will be in God. Ah, it is lovely.

"The Lord is that Spirit: and where the Spirit of the Lord is, there is liberty" (2 Corinthians 3:17).

Thought for today: If you would believe half as much as you ask, you would receive.

DAY 11

A LIFE OF PERFECT ACTIVITY

My God shall supply all your need according to
His riches in glory by Christ Jesus.
—Philippians 4:19

Scripture reading: Acts 5:14–42

Only believe! God will not fail you, beloved. It is impossible for God to fail. Believe God; rest in Him. The Bible is the most important book in the world. But some people have to be pressed in before they can be pressed on. Oh, this glorious inheritance of holy joy and faith, this glorious baptism in the Holy Spirit—it is a perfected place. *"All things are become new"* (2 Corinthians 5:17) because *"you are Christ's; and Christ is God's"* (1 Corinthians 3:23).

God means for us to walk in this royal way. When God opens a door, no man can shut it. (See Revelation 3:8.) John made a royal way, and Jesus walked in it. Jesus left us the responsibility of allowing Him to bring forth through us the greater works. (See John 14:12.) Jesus left His disciples with much, and with much more to be added until God receives us in that day.

When we receive power, we must stir ourselves up with the truth that we are responsible for the need around us. God will supply all our need so that the need of the needy may be met through us. God has given us a great indwelling force of power. If we do not step into our privileges, it is a tragedy.

There is no standing still. *"As He is, so are we in this world"* (1 John 4:17). *"We are the offspring of God"* (Acts 17:29), and we have divine impulses. After we have received, we will have power. We have been focusing too much on feeling the power. God is waiting for us to act. Jesus lived a life of perfect activity. He lived in the realm of divine appointment.

We must dare to press on until God comes forth in mighty power. May God give us the hearing of faith so that the power may come down like a cloud. Press on until Jesus is glorified and multitudes are gathered in.

Thought for today: God's rest is an undisturbed place where heaven bends to meet you.

DAY 12

THE COMFORT OF THE HOLY SPIRIT

I will pray the Father, and He shall give you another Comforter, that He may abide with you for ever.
—John 14:16

Scripture reading: John 14:15–31

Jesus knew that He was going away and that, if He went away, it was expedient, it was necessary, it was important that Another come in His place and continue guiding and teaching them as He had been. (See John 16:7, 14.) "*You in Me, and I in you*" (John 14:20). There was a plan of divine order; the Holy Spirit was to come.

I want you to see what has to take place when the Holy Spirit comes:

> *And I will pray the Father, and He shall give you another Comforter, that He may abide with you for ever; even the Spirit of truth; whom the world cannot receive, because it sees Him not, neither knows Him: but you know Him; for He dwells with you, and shall be in you. I will not leave you comfortless: I will come to you.* (John 14:16–18)

I don't know a word that could be as fitting at this time as this word "*Comforter.*" I want to take you with me into the coming of this Holy Spirit.

After Jesus ascended to heaven, He asked the Father to send the Comforter. It was a needy moment, a needy hour, a necessity. Why? Because the disciples would need comforting.

How could they be comforted? The Holy Spirit would take the word of Christ and reveal it to them. (See John 16:14.) What could help them as much as a word by the Spirit? For the Spirit is breath, is life, is person, is power. He gives the breath of Himself to us, the nature of Him. How beautiful that, when the Spirit came, He should be called the *"Spirit of truth"* (John 14:17). Oh, if we would only let that truth sink deep into our hearts!

Some people have wondered that if they were to ask for the baptism of the Holy Spirit, if an evil power could come instead or if an evil power could possess them while they were waiting for the Holy Spirit. No! When you receive the Holy Spirit, you receive the Spirit of Truth, the Spirit who gives revelation, the Spirit who takes the words of Jesus and makes them life to you. In your moment of need, He is the Comforter.

Thought for today: When the Holy Spirit comes into your body, He comes to unveil the King, to assure you of His presence.

DAY 13

THE WORK OF THE HOLY SPIRIT

He shall take of Mine, and shall show it to you.
—John 16:15

Scripture reading: John 16:5–15

What will the Holy Spirit do? The Holy Spirit is prophetic. He says, *"Be of good cheer"* (John 16:33); *"Take My yoke upon you, and learn of Me"* (Matthew 11:29); *"Have peace one with another"* (Mark 9:50). You say, "But that is what Jesus said." It is what the Holy Spirit is taking and revealing to us. The Holy Spirit is the spokesman in these days, and He speaks the Word. The Holy Spirit takes the words of Jesus, and He is so full of truth that He never adds anything to them. He gives you the unadulterated Word of Truth, the Word of Life.

What are His words? Truths like these: *"I am the light of the world"* (John 8:12); *"For God sent not His Son into the world to condemn the world; but that the world through Him might be saved"* (John 3:17); and *"Come to Me, all you who labor and are heavy laden, and I will give you rest"* (Matthew 11:28). The Holy Spirit takes these words and gives them to you.

The Holy Spirit, the Spirit of Truth, is bringing forth the Word of Life. *"I will give you rest."* Rest? Oh, there is no rest like it! It can come in your moment of greatest trial.

When my dear wife was lying dead, the doctors could do nothing, and they said to me, "She is done; we cannot help you." My heart was so moved, and I said, "O God, I can't spare her!"

I went up to her and I said, "Oh, come back; come back and speak to me. Come back, come back!"

And the Spirit of the Lord moved, and she came back and smiled again.

Then the Holy Spirit said to me, "She is mine. Her work is done; she is mine."

Oh, the comforting word! No one else could have done it, but the Comforter came. At that moment, my dear wife passed away.

Thought for today: The Comforter has a word for us this day. There is only one Comforter, and He has been with the Father from the beginning. He comes only to give light.

DAY 14

BE SPECIFIC IN WHAT YOU ASK

One thing have I desired of the Lord, that will I seek after.
—Psalm 27:4

Scripture reading: Psalm 27

The person who says "I am ready for anything" will never get it. "What are you seeking, my brother?" "Oh, I am ready for anything." You will never get *anything*.

When the Lord reveals to you that you must be filled with the Holy Spirit, seek only that one thing, and God will give you that one thing. It is necessary for you to seek one thing first.

Never forget, the baptism will always be as it was in the beginning. It has not changed. And if you want a real baptism, expect it to be just the same as the early believers had it at the beginning.

"What did they have at the beginning?" you ask.

Well, they knew when others had the same experience they had had at the beginning, for they heard them speak in tongues. That is the only way they did know, because they heard the others saying the same things in the Spirit that they had said at the beginning. As it was in the beginning, so it will be forever.

I do not say anything against ordination; I think that is very good. However, there is an ordination that is better, and it is the ordination with the King. This is the only ordination that is going to equip you for the future.

The person who has passed through that ordination goes forth with fresh feet that have been prepared by the gospel (see Ephesians 6:15); he goes forth with a fresh voice, speaking as the Spirit gives utterance (see

Acts 2:4); he goes forth with a fresh mind that's been illuminated by the power of God (see Hebrews 8:10); he goes forth with a fresh vision and sees all things new (see 2 Corinthians 5:17).

When the Holy Spirit comes, He will reveal things to you. Has He revealed them yet? He is going to do it. Just expect Him to do so. The best thing for you is to expect Him to do it now.

Thought for today: The King is already on His throne, but He needs crowning; when the Holy Spirit comes, He crowns the King inside of us.

DAY 15

OVERCOMING HINDRANCES

They were all filled with the Holy Spirit and began to speak with other tongues.
—Acts 2:4 (NKJV)

Scripture reading: Acts 2:1–41

Expect any manifestation of the Spirit when you are coming through into the baptism. As far as I am concerned, you can have the biggest time on earth; you can scream as much as you like. Yet some people are wary of how they will react.

A woman in Switzerland came to me after I had helped her and asked to speak to me further. "Now that I feel I am healed," she said, "and that terrible carnal passion that has bound and hindered me is gone, I feel that I have a new mind. I believe I would like to receive the Holy Spirit, but when I hear these people screaming, I feel like running away."

After that, we were at another meeting in Switzerland where a large hotel was joined to the building. At the close of one of the morning services, the power of God fell—that is the only way I can describe it, the power of God *fell*. This poor, timid creature who couldn't bear to hear anybody scream, screamed so loud that all the waiters in this big hotel came out with their aprons on and with their trays to see what was up. Nothing was especially up. Something had come down, and it had so altered the situation that this woman could stand anything after that.

When God begins dealing with you on the baptism, He begins on this line: He starts with the things that are the most difficult. He starts with your fear; He starts with your human nature. He puts the fear away; He gets the human nature out of the way. And just as you dissolve, just as the power of the Spirit brings a dissolving to your human nature, in the same act the Holy Spirit flows into the place where you are being dissolved, and you are quickened just where you come into death.

Thought for today: As you die—naturally, humanly, carnally, selfishly—to every evil thing, the new life, the Holy Spirit, floods the whole condition until you become transformed.

DAY 16

YOU HAVE AN ANOINTING

But you have an anointing from the Holy One.
—1 John 2:20 (NKJV)

Scripture reading: 1 John 2:15–29

Another role of the Holy Spirit that is necessary for today we find in John 14:26:

> *But the Helper, the Holy Spirit, whom the Father will send in My name, He will teach you all things, and bring to your remembrance all things that I said to you.* (NKJV)

Jesus said something very similar in a later chapter: *"He shall receive of Mine, and shall show it to you"* (John 16:14). Everything that has been revealed to you was first taken. So, first, the Holy Spirit takes of what is Christ's and reveals it to you. Then you come to the place where you need another touch. What is it? In the necessity of your ministry, He will bring to your remembrance everything that you need in your ministry. That is an important thing for preachers. God will give us His Word, and if there is anything special we need, He will bring that to our memories, too. The Holy Spirit comes to bring the Word to our remembrance.

I will throw this word out to you as a help for future reflection: *"You shall receive power"* (Acts 1:8). Oh, may God grant that we will not forget it!

What do I mean by that? Many people, instead of standing on the rock-solid word of faith and believing that they have received the baptism with its anointing and power, say, "Oh, if I could only feel that I have received it!"

Very often, your feelings are a place of discouragement. You have to get away from relying on human feelings or desires. Earthly desires are not

God's desires. All thoughts of holiness, all thoughts of purity, all thoughts of power from the Holy Spirit are from above. Human thoughts are like clouds that belong to the earth. *"For My thoughts are not your thoughts"* (Isaiah 55:8).

Thought for today: Your feelings rob you of your greatest place of anointing.

DAY 17

A POWERFUL ANOINTING

God anointed Jesus…with the Holy Spirit and with power.
—Acts 10:38 (NKJV)

Scripture reading: Acts 10:24–48

Suppose that all around me are people with needs: a woman is dying; a man has lost all the powers of his faculties; another person is apparently dying. Here they are. I see the great need, and I drop down on my knees and cry. Yet in doing so, I miss it all.

God does not want me to cry. God does not want me to labor. God does not want me to anguish and to be filled with anxiety and a sorrowful spirit. What does He want me to do? Only believe. After you have received, only believe. Come to the authority of it; dare to believe. Say, "I will do it!"

So the baptism of the Holy Spirit says to me, "*You have an anointing*" (1 John 2:20 NKJV). The anointing has come; the anointing remains; the anointing is with us. But what if you have not lived in the place in which the unction, the anointing, can be increased? Then the Spirit is grieved; then you are not moved. You are like one who is dead. You feel that all the joy is gone.

What is the matter? There is something between you and the Holy One; you are not clean, not pure, not desirous of Him alone. Something else has come in the way. Then the Spirit is grieved, and you have lost the unction.

Is the Unctioner still there? Yes. When He comes in, He comes to remain. He will either be grieved, full of groaning and travail, or He will be there to lift you above the powers of darkness, transform you by His power, and take you to a place where you may be fully equipped.

Many people lose all potential positions of attainment because they fail to understand this:

> *But the anointing which you have received of Him abides in you, and you need not that any man teach you: but as the same anointing teaches you of all things, and is truth, and is no lie, and even as it has taught you, you shall abide in Him.* (1 John 2:27)

What *"anointing"* is referred to here? The same anointing from God that anointed Jesus is with you, *"and you need not that any man teach you."* The same anointing will teach you all things.

O lovely Jesus! Blessed Incarnation of holy display! Thank God for the Trinity displayed in our hearts today. Thank God for this glorious open way. Thank God for life all along the way. Praise God for hope that we may all be changed today. Hallelujah!

> Peace, peace, sweet peace,
> Coming down from the Father above,
> Peace, peace, wonderful peace,
> Sweet peace, the gift of God's love.

This is the very position and presence that will bring everybody into a fullness.

Thought for today: Thank God for darkness that is turning into day.

DAY 18

THE MORE EXCELLENT WAY

Pursue love.
—1 Corinthians 14:1 (NKJV)

Scripture reading: 1 Corinthians 13

When love is in perfect operation, all other things will work in harmony, for prophetic utterances are of no value unless they are perfectly covered with divine love. Our Lord Jesus would never have accomplished His great plan in this world except that He was so full of love for His Father, and love for us, that His love never failed to accomplish its purpose.

I believe that His love will have to come into our lives. Christ must be the summit, the desire, the plan of all things. All our sayings, doings, and workings must be well pleasing in and to Him, and then our prophetic utterances will be a blessing through God; they will never be side issues. There is no imitation in a man filled with the Holy Spirit. Imitation is lost as the great plan of Christ becomes the ideal of his life.

God wants you to be balanced in spiritual anointing so that you will always do what pleases Him and not what will please other people or yourself. The ideal must be that all you do will be edifying, and your primary purpose will be to please the Lord.

When someone came to Moses and said that there were two others in the camp prophesying, Moses said, *"Would God that all the LORD's people were prophets"* (Numbers 11:29). This is a clear revelation along these lines that God wants us to be in such a spiritual, holy place that He could take our words and so fill them with divine power that we would speak only as the Spirit leads in prophetic utterances.

Beloved, there is spiritual language, and there is also human language, which always stays on the human plane. The divine comes into the same language so that it is changed by spiritual power and brings life to those who hear you speak. But this divine touch of prophecy will never come in any way except through the infilling of the Spirit.

Thought for today: If you wish to be anything for God, do not miss His plan.

DAY 19

SPEECH THAT EDIFIES

And it shall come to pass afterward, that I will pour out My Spirit upon all flesh; and your sons and your daughters shall prophesy, your old men shall dream dreams, your young men shall see visions: and also upon the servants and upon the handmaids in those days will I pour out My Spirit.
—Joel 2:28–29

Scripture reading: 1 Corinthains 14:1–25

We know that the prophecy spoken by Joel was fulfilled on the day of Pentecost. This was the first outpouring of the Spirit, but what would it be like now if we would only wake up to the words of our Master, "*Greater works than these shall he do; because I go to My Father*" (John 14:12)?

Hear what the Scripture says to us: "*However when He, the Spirit of truth, is come, He will guide you into all truth: for He shall not speak of Himself; but whatsoever He shall hear, that shall He speak*" (John 16:13). The Holy Spirit is inspiration; the Holy Spirit is revelation; the Holy Spirit is manifestation; the Holy Spirit is operation. When a man comes into the fullness of the Holy Spirit, he is in perfect order, built up on scriptural foundations.

I have failed to see anyone understand 1 Corinthians 12–14 unless he has been baptized with the Holy Spirit. He may talk about the Holy Spirit and the gifts, but his understanding is only a superficial one. However, when he gets baptized with the Holy Spirit, he speaks about a deep inward conviction by the power of the Spirit working in him, a revelation of that Scripture. On the other hand, there is so much that a man receives when he is born again. He receives the first love and has a revelation of Jesus. "*But if we walk in the light, as He is in the light, we have fellowship one with another, and the blood of Jesus Christ His Son cleanses us from all sin"* (1 John 1:7).

But God wants a man to be on fire so that he will always speak as an oracle of God. He wants to so build that man on the foundations of God that everyone who sees and hears him will say he is a new man after the order of the Spirit. *"Old things are passed away; behold, all things are become new"* (2 Corinthians 5:17). New things have come, and he is now in the divine order. When a man is filled with the Holy Spirit, he has a vital power that makes people know he has seen God. He ought to be in such a place spiritually that when he goes into a neighbor's house, or out among people, they will feel that God has come into their midst.

"He that prophesies speaks to men to edification, and exhortation, and comfort. He that speaks in an unknown tongue edifies himself; but he that prophesies edifies the church" (1 Corinthians 14:3–4). There are two edifications spoken of here. Which is the first? To edify yourself. After you have been edified by the Spirit, you are able to edify the church through the Spirit. What we need is more of the Holy Spirit. O beloved, it is not merely a measure of the Spirit, it is a pressed-down measure. It is not merely a pressed-down measure, it is *"shaken together, and running over"* (Luke 6:38). Praise the Lord!

Thought for today: Anybody can hold a full cup, but you cannot hold an overflowing cup, and the baptism of the Holy Spirit is an overflowing cup.

DAY 20

THREE WITNESSES TO THE BAPTISM

And now why tarriest you? arise, and be baptized, and wash away your sins, calling on the name of the Lord.
—Acts 22:16

Scripture reading: Galatians 3:1–14

I want to take you to the Scriptures to prove my position that tongues are the evidence of the baptism in the Holy Spirit. Businessmen know that in cases of law where there are two clear witnesses, they could win a case before any judge. On the clear evidence of two witnesses, any judge will give a verdict. What has God given us? He has given us three clear witnesses on the baptism in the Holy Spirit—more than are necessary in law courts.

The first is in Acts 2:4, on the day of Pentecost: "*They were all filled with the Holy Spirit and began to speak with other tongues, as the Spirit gave them utterance*" (NKJV).

Here we have the original pattern. And God gave to Peter an eternal word that couples this experience with the promise that came before it: "*This is what was spoken by the prophet Joel*" (Acts 2:16 NKJV). God wants you to have this—nothing less than this. He wants you to receive the baptism in the Holy Spirit according to this original Pentecostal pattern.

In Acts 10, we have another witness. Cornelius had had a vision of a holy angel and had sent for Peter. When Peter arrived and proclaimed the gospel message, the Holy Spirit fell on all those who heard his words.

> *And those of the circumcision who believed were astonished, as many as came with Peter, because the gift of the Holy Spirit had been poured out on the Gentiles also.* (Acts 10:45 NKJV)

What convinced these prejudiced Jews that the Holy Spirit had come? *"For they heard them speak with tongues and magnify God"* (v. 46 NKJV). There was no other way for them to know. This evidence could not be contradicted. It is the biblical evidence.

If some people were to have an angel come and talk to them as Cornelius did, they would say that they knew they were baptized. Do not be fooled by anything.

We have heard two witnesses. Now let us look at Acts 19:6, which records Paul ministering to certain disciples in Ephesus: *"And when Paul had laid hands on them, the Holy Spirit came upon them, and they spoke with tongues and prophesied"* (NKJV).

These Ephesians received the identical biblical evidence that the apostles had received at the beginning, and they prophesied in addition. Three times the Scriptures show us this evidence of the baptism in the Spirit. I do not glorify tongues. No, by God's grace, I glorify the Giver of tongues. And above all, I glorify Him whom the Holy Spirit has come to reveal to us, the Lord Jesus Christ. It is He who sends the Holy Spirit, and I glorify Him because He makes no distinction between us and those who believed at the beginning.

But what are tongues for? Look at the second verse of 1 Corinthians 14, and you will see a very blessed truth: *"For he that speaks in an unknown tongue speaks not to men, but to God: for no man understands him; however in the spirit he speaks mysteries."* Oh, hallelujah! Have you been there, beloved? I tell you, God wants to take you there. The passage goes on to say, *"He that speaks in an unknown tongue edifies himself"* (v. 4).

Enter into the promises of God. It is your inheritance. I pray that you may be so filled with Him that it will not be possible for you to move without a revival of some kind resulting.

Thought for today: Be sure that what you receive is according to the Word of God.

DAY 21

RECEIVING THE BAPTISM

You shall receive power when the Holy Spirit has come upon you.
—Acts 1:8 (NKJV)

Scripture reading: Acts 1:1–11

I believe God wants us to know more about the baptism of the Holy Spirit. And I believe that God wants us to know the truth in such a way that we may all have a clear understanding of what He means when He desires all His people to receive the Holy Spirit.

Jesus, our Mediator and Advocate, was filled with the Holy Spirit. He commanded His followers concerning these days we are in and gave instructions about the time through the Holy Spirit. I can see that if we are going to accomplish anything, we are going to accomplish it because we are under the power of the Holy Spirit.

During my lifetime, I have seen lots of satanic forces, Spiritualists, and all other "ists." I tell you that there is a power that is satanic, and there is a power that is the Holy Spirit. I remember that after we received the Holy Spirit and when people were speaking in tongues as the Spirit gave utterance—we don't know the Holy Spirit in any other way—the Spiritualists heard about it and came to the meeting in good time to fill two rows of seats.

When the power of God fell upon us, these imitators began their shaking and moving, with utterances from the satanic forces. The Spirit of the Lord was mighty upon me. I went to them and said, "Now, you demons, clear out of here!" And out they went. I followed them right out into the street, and then they turned around and cursed me. It made no difference; they were out.

I implore you to hear that the baptism in the Holy Spirit is to possess us so that we are, and may be continually, so full of the Holy Spirit that utterances and revelations and eyesight and everything else may be so remarkably controlled by the Spirit of God that we live and move in this glorious sphere of usefulness for the glory of God.

Thought for today: There is a fullness of God where all other powers must cease to be.

DAY 22

ENTERING A NEW REALM

He that believes on the Son of God has the witness in himself.
—1 John 5:10

Scripture reading: 1 John 5

If you are a businessman, you need to be baptized in the Holy Spirit. For any kind of business, you need to know the power of the Holy Spirit, because if you are not baptized with the Holy Spirit, Satan has a tremendous power to interfere with the progress of your life. If you come into the baptism of the Holy Spirit, there is a new realm for your business.

I remember one day being in London at a meeting. About eleven o'clock, they said to me, "We will have to close the meeting. We are not allowed to have this place any later than eleven o'clock." There were several who were under the power of the Spirit. A man rose up and looked at me, saying, "Oh, don't leave me, please. I feel that I do not dare be left. I must receive the Holy Spirit. Will you go home with us?" "Yes," I said, "I will go." His wife was there as well. They were two hungry people just being awakened by the power of the Spirit to know that they were lacking in their lives and that they needed the power of God.

In about an hour's time, we arrived at their big, beautiful house in the country. It was wintertime. He began stirring the fire up and putting coal on, and he said, "We will soon have a tremendous fire, so we will get warmed. Then we will have a big supper." And I suppose the next thing would have been going to bed.

"No, thank you," I said. "I have not come here for your supper or for your bed. I thought you wanted me to come with you so that you might receive the Holy Spirit."

"Oh," he replied. "Will you pray with us?"

"I have come for nothing else." I knew I could keep myself warm in a prayer meeting without a fire.

About half past three in the morning, his wife was as full as could be, speaking in tongues. God was doing wonderful things that night. I went to the end of the table. There he was, groaning terribly. So I said, "Your wife has received the Holy Spirit." "Oh," he said, "this is going to be a big night for me." I tell you, you also will have big nights like this man had, whether you receive the baptism or not, if you will seek God with all your heart.

I often say there is more done in the seeking than in any other way. We have to get to a place where we know that unless we meet face-to-face with God and get all the crooked places out of our lives, there will be no room for the Holy Spirit, for the indwelling presence of God. But when God gets a chance at us, and by the vision of the blood of Jesus we see ourselves as God sees us, then we have a revelation. Without this, we are undone and helpless.

At five o'clock in the morning, this man stood up and said, "I am through." He was not baptized. "I am settled," he continued. "God has settled me. Now I must have a few hours' rest before I go to my business at eight o'clock."

My word! That was quite a day at his business. In many years, he had never lived a day like that. He went about his business among all his men, and they said, "What is up with the man? What is up with the boss? What has taken place? Oh, what a change!"

The whole place was electrified. Formerly he had been like a great big lion prowling about, but God had touched him. The touch of Omnipotence had broken this man down until right there in his business the men were broken up in his presence. Oh, I tell you, there is something in pursuing; there is something in waiting. What is it? It is this: God slays a man so that he may begin on a new plane in his life.

That night, at about ten o'clock, he was baptized in the Holy Spirit in a meeting. A short time afterward, when I was passing through the grounds toward this man's house, his two sons rushed out to where I was, threw their arms around me, and kissed me, saying, "You have sent us a new father."

Thought for today: God turns lions into lambs.

DAY 23

THE BAPTISM IS RESURRECTION

That I may know Hiim, and the power of His resurrection.
—Philippians 3:10

Scripture reading: Philippians 3

The power of the Holy Spirit creates new men and new women. The Holy Spirit takes away stony hearts and gives hearts of flesh. (See Ezekiel 36:26–27.) And when God gets His way like that, there is a tremendous shaking among the dry bones. (See Ezekiel 37:4–10.)

We must see that we are no good unless God takes charge of us. But when He has real control of us, our future takes on a new outlook. What a wonderful open door of opportunities for God to use us!

Beloved, we must seek this ideal by the Spirit. What should we do? We do not dare to do anything but go through and receive the baptism. Submit to the power of God. If you yield, other people are saved. You will die unless you have a power of resurrection, a touch for others. But if you live only for God, then other people will be raised out of death and all kinds of evil into a blessed life through the Spirit.

We must see that this baptism of the Spirit is greater than everything. You can say what you like, do as you like, but until you have the Holy Spirit, you won't know what the resurrection touch is. Resurrection is by the power of the Spirit. And remember, when I talk about resurrection, I am talking about one of the greatest things in the Scriptures. Resurrection is evidence that we have awakened with a new line of truth that cannot cease to be but will always go on with a greater force and increasing power with God.

Remember that the baptism of the Holy Spirit is resurrection. If you can touch this ideal of God with its resurrection power, you will see that nothing earthly can remain; you will see that all disease will clear out. If you get filled with the Holy Spirit, all satanic forces that cause fits, all these lame legs, all these foot afflictions, all these kidney troubles, and all these nervous, fearful things will go. *Resurrection* is the word for it. Resurrection shakes away death and breathes life in you; it lets you know that you are quickened from the dead by the Spirit and that you are made like Jesus. Glory to God!

Oh, the word *resurrection*! I wish I could say it on the same level as the word *Jesus*. They very harmoniously go together.

Thought for today: Jesus is resurrection, and to know Jesus in this resurrection power is to see that you no longer have to be dead; you are alive unto God by the Spirit.

DAY 24

A NEW DAY

Behold, I will do a new thing; now it shall spring forth; shall you not know it? I will even make a way in the wilderness, and rivers in the desert.
—Isaiah 43:19

Scripture reading: Revelation 21

See to it that today you press on with a new order of the Spirit so that you can never be where you were before. This is a new day for us all. You say, "What about the people who are already baptized in the Spirit?" Oh, this is a new day also for those who have been baptized, for the Spirit is an unlimited source of power. He is in no way stationary. God has no place for a person who is stationary. The man who is going to catch the fire, hold forth the truth, and always be on the watchtower is the one who is going to be a beacon for all saints, having a light greater than he would have naturally. He must see that God's grace, God's life, and God's Spirit are a million times mightier than he.

The man who is baptized in the Holy Spirit is baptized into a new order altogether. You cannot ever be ordinary after that. You are on an extraordinary plane; you are brought into line with the mind of God. You have come into touch with ideals in every way.

If you want oratory, it is in the baptism of the Spirit. If you want the touch of quickened sense that moves your body until you know that you are completely renewed, it is by the Holy Spirit. And while I say so much about the Holy Spirit, I withdraw everything that doesn't put Jesus in the place He belongs. For when I speak about the Holy Spirit, it is always with reference to revelations of Jesus. The Holy Spirit is the Revealer of the mighty Christ who possesses everything for us so that we may never know any weakness. All limitations are gone. And you are now in a place where God has taken the ideal and moved you on with His own velocity, which has a speed beyond all human mind and thought. Glory to God!

Thought for today: Nothing in God is stationary.

DAY 25

HIGHER HEIGHTS

I will declare Your name to My brethren,
in the midst of the church will I sing praise to You.
—Hebrews 2:12

Scripture reading: Hebrews 2:1–13

The Spirit of the Lord must have His way in everything. Oh, what would happen if we would all loosen up! Sometimes I think it is almost necessary to give an address to those who are already baptized in the Holy Spirit. I feel that, just like the Corinthian church, we may have, as it were, gifts and graces, and we may use them all, but we sit in them and do not go on beyond where we are.

I maintain that all gifts and graces are only for one thing: to make you desire gifts and graces. Don't miss what I say. Every touch of the divine life by the Spirit is only for one purpose: to make your life go on to a higher height than where you are. Beloved, if anybody has to rise up in the meeting to tell me how they were baptized with the Holy Spirit in order for me to know they are baptized, I say, "You have fallen from grace. You ought to have such a baptism that everybody can tell you are baptized without your telling how you were baptized." That would make a new day. That would be a sermon in itself to everybody, not only in here but also outside. Then people would follow you to get to know where you have come from and where you are going. (See John 3:8.) You say, "I want that. I won't settle until I get that." God will surely give it to you.

The Holy Spirit can only come into us (His temples) when we are fully yielded to Him, for the Spirit *"dwells not in temples made with hands"* (Acts 7:48) but in *"fleshy tables of the heart"* (2 Corinthians 3:3). So it doesn't matter what kind of a building you get; you cannot count on the building being a substitute for the Holy Spirit. You will all have to be temples of the Holy Spirit for the building to be anything like Holy Spirit order.

Thought for today: The Holy Spirit never comes until there is a place ready for Him.

DAY 26

RECEIVE THE SPIRIT

I thank You, O Father, Lord of heaven and earth,
because You have hidden these things from the wise and prudent,
and have revealed them to babes.
—Matthew 11:25

Scripture reading: Matthew 19:13–30

I wonder how many people today are prepared to be baptized. Oh, you say you couldn't be baptized? Then you have been an adult too long. You need to become childlike again. Do you know that there is a difference between being a baby and anything else in the world?

Many people have been waiting for years for the baptism, and what has been the problem? What is the wise man's difficulty? A wise man is too careful. And while he is in the operation of the Spirit, he wants to know what he is saying. No man can know what he is saying when the Spirit is upon him. His own mind is inactive. If you get into that place in which you are near God, the mind of Christ comes by the power of the Spirit. Under these conditions, Christ prays and speaks in the Spirit through you as the Spirit gives utterance. It is the mind and plan of God for us to receive the Holy Spirit.

The natural man cannot receive the Spirit of God. (See 1 Corinthians 2:14.) But when you get into a supernatural place, then you receive the mind of God. Again, what is the difference between a *"wise and prudent"* man and a baby? The man drinks cautiously, but the baby swallows it all, and the mother has to hold the bottle, or some of that will go down, too. This is how God wants it to be in the Spirit. The spiritually minded baby cannot walk, but God walks in him. The spiritually minded baby cannot talk, but God talks through him. The spiritually minded baby cannot dress himself, but God dresses him and clothes him with His righteousness.

Oh, beloved, if we can only be infants in this way today, great things will take place along the lines and thought of the Spirit of God. The Lord wants us all to be so like-minded with Him that He can put His seal upon us.

Does the baby ever lose his intelligence? Does he ever lose his common sense? Does the baby who comes into the will of God lose his reason or his credentials in any way? No, God will increase your abilities and help you in everything. I am not talking here about just being a baby. I am talking about being a baby in the Spirit. Paul said in 1 Corinthians 14:20, *"In malice be you children, but in understanding be men,"* and I believe the Spirit desires to breathe through all the attributes of the Spirit so that we may understand what the mind of the Lord is concerning us in the Holy Spirit.

Thought for today: If you will become childlike enough, if you will yield to God and let the Spirit have His way, God will fill you with the Holy Spirit.

DAY 27

WHAT ABOUT MANIFESTATIONS?

But the manifestation of the Spirit is given to every man to profit withal.
—1 Corinthians 12:7

Scripture reading: 1 Corinthians 12:1–11

We must never transgress because of liberty. What I mean is this: it would be wrong for me to take opportunities just because the Spirit of the Lord is upon me. But it would be perfectly justifiable if I clearly allow the Spirit of the Lord to have His liberty with me. However, we are not to behave inappropriately in our liberty, for the flesh is more extravagant than the Spirit.

The Spirit's extravagances are always for edification, strengthening character, and bringing us all more into conformity with the life of Christ. But fleshly extravagances always mar these things and bring the saints into a place of trial for the moment. As the Spirit of the Lord takes further hold of a person, we may get liberty in it, but we are tried through the manifestations of it.

I believe we have come to a liberty of the Spirit that is so pure it will never bring a frown of distraction over another person's mind. I have seen many people who were in the power of the Spirit, but they exhibited a manifestation that was not foundational or even helpful. I have seen people under the mighty power of the Holy Spirit who have waved their hands wildly and moved on the floor and gone on in such a state that no one could say the body was not under the power. However, there was more natural power than spiritual power there, and the natural condition of the person, along with the spiritual condition, caused the manifestation. Though we know the Spirit of the Lord was there, the manifestation was not something that would elevate or please the people or grant them a desire for more of that. It wasn't an edification of the Spirit.

If there are any here who have those manifestations, I want to help you. I don't want to hurt you. It is good that you should have the Spirit upon you; people need to be filled with the Spirit. But you never have a right to say you couldn't help doing this, that, or the other manifestation.

No manifestation of the body ever glorifies the Lord except the tongue. If you seek to be free in the operation of the Spirit through the mouth, then the tongue, which may be under a kind of subconscious control by the Spirit, brings out the glory of the Lord, and that will always bring edification, consolation, and comfort.

No other manifestation will do this. Still, I believe that it is necessary to have all these other manifestations when someone is filled with the Spirit for the first time. When the Spirit is there, the flesh must find some way out, and so, through past experience, we allow all these things at the beginning. But I believe the Holy Spirit brings a sound condition of mind, and the first thing must pass away so that the divine position may remain.

And so there are various manifestations, including kicking and waving, that take place at the incoming of the Holy Spirit, when the flesh and the Spirit are in conflict. One must decrease and die, and the other must increase and multiply. Consequently, when you come to understand this, you are in a place of sound judgment and know that now the Holy Spirit has come to take you on with God.

When the Holy Spirit is allowed full reign over the operation of human life, He always works out of divine wisdom. And when He gets perfect control of a life, the divine source flows through so that all the people may receive edification in the Spirit. If you act foolishly after you have had wisdom taught you, nobody will give you much leeway.

"We then that are strong ought to bear the infirmities of the weak" (Romans 15:1). Some who come to church services know nothing about the power of the Holy Spirit. They get saved and are quickened, and after the Spirit comes upon them, you will see all these manifestations. In love and grace, you should bear with them as newborn babes in the Spirit and rejoice with them because that is only a beginning to an end. The Lord wouldn't want us to be anything but *"strong in the Lord, and in the power of His might"* (Ephesians 6:10) to help everyone around us.

Thought for today: Liberty is beautiful when we never use it to satisfy ourselves but use it in the Lord.

DAY 28

OUR HELPER

No one can say that Jesus is Lord except by the Holy Spirit.
—1 Corinthians 12:3 (NKJV)

Scripture reading: John 14:16–31

The Holy Spirit has a royal plan, a heavenly plan. He came to unveil the King, to show the character of God, to unveil the precious blood. Since I have the Holy Spirit within me, I see Jesus clothed for humanity. He was moved by the Spirit and led by the Spirit. We read of some who heard the Word but did not benefit from it because faith was lacking in them. (See Romans 9:6–8.) We must have a living faith in God's Word, a faith that is quickened by the Spirit.

A man may be saved and still have a human spirit. In many people who hear about the baptism of the Holy Spirit, the human spirit immediately arises against the Holy Spirit. The human spirit is not subject to the law of God, nor can it be. (See Romans 8:7.) The disciples at one time wanted to call down fire from heaven, and Jesus said to them, *"You know not what manner of spirit you are of"* (Luke 9:55). The human spirit is not subject to the law of God.

The Holy Spirit came forth for one purpose: to reveal Jesus to us. Jesus *"made Himself of no reputation"* (Philippians 2:7), and He was *"obedient to death"* (v. 8), that God should forever hold Him up as a token of submissive yieldedness. God highly exalted Him and gave Him a name above every name. *"Now He that has wrought us for the self-same thing is God, who also has given to us the earnest of the Spirit"* (2 Corinthians 5:5). With the clothing upon of the Spirit, human depravity is covered, and everything that is contrary to the mind of God is destroyed. God must have bodies for Himself, perfectly prepared by the Holy Spirit, for the day of the Lord. *"For in this we groan, earnestly desiring to be clothed upon with our house which is from heaven"* (v. 2).

Was Paul speaking here about the coming of the Lord? No! Yet this condition of preparedness is highly relevant. The Holy Spirit is coming to take back a church and a perfect bride. The Holy Spirit must find in us perfect yieldedness, with every human desire subjected to Him. "*No one can say that Jesus is Lord except by the Holy Spirit*" (1 Corinthians 12:3 NKJV). He has come to reveal Christ in us, so that the glorious flow of the life of God may bring rivers of living water to the thirsty land within.

The Spirit has to breathe into us a new occupancy, a new order. The Holy Spirit came to give the vision of a life in which Jesus is perfected. It is Christ "*who has saved us, and called us with a holy calling, not according to our works, but according to His own purpose and grace*" (2 Timothy 1:9).

We who are saved have been called with a holy calling, called to be saints—to be pure, holy, and Godlike; to be sons with power. It is a long time now since it was settled and death was abolished. Death has no more power. This was made known through the gospel, which brought in immortality. Mortality is a hindrance. Sin has no more dominion over you. You reign in Christ, and you make rightful use of His finished work. Don't groan and travail for a week. If you are in need, "*only believe*" (Mark 5:36). Don't fast to get some special thing, "*only believe.*" It is according to your faith that God blesses you with more faith. "*Have faith in God*" (Mark 11:22). If you are free in God, believe! Believe, and it will be unto you even as you believe. (See Matthew 9:29.)

"*Awake you that sleep*" (Ephesians 5:14); put on light, and open your eyes. "*If you then be risen with Christ, seek those things which are above, where Christ sits on the right hand of God*" (Colossians 3:1). Stir yourselves up, beloved! Where are you? I am risen with Christ, planted in Him. It was a beautiful planting. I am seated with Him. God gives me the credit, and I believe Him. Why should I doubt?

Dare to believe until the life of Jesus is implanted within your soul. "*The righteous also shall hold on his way*" (Job 17:9). God has reserved him who is godly for Himself. (See Psalm 4:3.) Therefore, lift up your heads.

Thought for today: The devil makes you remember the day you failed, though you would give the world to forget about it. But God has forgotten when He forgives.

DAY 29

NO CONDEMNATION

There is...now no condemnation to them which are in Christ Jesus, who walk not after the flesh, but after the Spirit.
—Romans 8:1

Scripture reading: Romans 8:1–17

Nothing is going to help you attain spiritual maturity or live this higher life, except divine life, which will always help you if you yield yourself absolutely to it. Not only are we exercised by this divine life, but also we are kept in perfect rest. It is needed in this day, for people everywhere are becoming satisfied with natural things. There is no definite cry or prayer within the soul that is making people stop and cry out for God and the coming of the Son.

I am intensely eager that by some means I may inspire you to see what the Spirit has for you. Life in Christ is absolutely different from death. Life is what people long for because of its possibilities; death is what people draw back from because of its finality. God has designed for us to live in freedom from the law of sin and death.

This truth is from the divine mind of the Master. He said that He who lives for himself will die. He who seeks to live will die, but he who is willing to die will live. (See Luke 17:33.) God wants us to see that there is a life that is contrary to this life.

The Spirit of the Lord reveals the following to us in the Word of God: *"He that believes on the Son has everlasting life: and he that believes not the Son shall not see life"* (John 3:36). The unbelieving person is living and walking about but not seeing life. There is a life that is always brought into condemnation, which is living in death. There is a life that is free from condemnation—living in the Life.

The plan of God's Son for us is to be so much greater in this world than we have ever comprehended. God's plan is not for me to stay where I was yesterday.

He desires that spiritual revelation will bring me into touch with divine harmony. God wants me to reach for something more. My eyes are looking up; my heart is looking up. My heart is big and enlarged in the presence of God, for I want to hear one word from God: "Come up higher." God will give us that—the privilege of going higher into a holy relationship with Him.

The person who is under no condemnation has the heavens opened above him. This person has the smile of God upon him. This person has come into the realm of faith and joy and knows that his prayers are answered. God the Holy Spirit would have us to understand that there is a place in the Holy Spirit where there is no condemnation. This place is holiness, purity, righteousness, higher ground, perfection, and being more perfected in the presence of God. This higher ground is perfection, where God is bringing us to live in such a way that He may smile through us and act upon us until our bodies become a flame of light ignited by Omnipotence. This is God's plan for us in the inheritance; this divine place is for us today.

There is no condemnation. God wants us to see our covering, that blessed assurance of being strengthened, that knowledge of the Rock of Ages cleft for me, that place where I know I am! And that joy unbounding where I know there are neither devils nor angels nor principalities nor powers to interfere with that life in Christ! (See Romans 8:38–39.) It is wonderful!

"No weapon that is formed against you shall prosper" (Isaiah 54:17). The power of the Most High God has put us in Christ. If we had put ourselves in, it would have been different. We were in the world, but God took us out of the world and put us into Christ. God today by His Spirit wants us to see how this regenerative power, this glorious principle of God's high thoughtfulness, is for us. God wants us to lose ourselves in His sweetness. There is a glorious power behind us when God is behind us; there is a wonderful going before when He goes before us. He said, "I will go before you, and I will be your rear guard." (See Isaiah 52:12.) And so, I see that God the Holy Spirit wants me today to penetrate, or bring forth, or show forth the glorious joy that is in this wonderful incarnation of the Spirit for us all in Christ Jesus. Glory to God!

Thought for today: God makes us devil-proof.

DAY 30

GOD'S GIFT FOR EVERYONE

He that believes on Me, as the scripture has said,
out of his belly shall flow rivers of living water.
—John 7:38

Scripture reading: John 4:1–14

God wants to help us see that every child of God ought to receive the Holy Spirit. Beloved, God wants us to understand that this is not difficult when we are in the right order. I want you to see what it means to seek the Holy Spirit.

If we were to examine John's Gospel, we would see that Jesus predicted all that we are getting today with the coming of the Holy Spirit. Our Lord said that the Holy Spirit would take of the things of His Word and reveal them to us. (See John 14:26; 16:14.) He would live out in us all of the life of Jesus.

If we could only think of what this really means! It is one of the ideals. Talk about graduation! Come into the graduation of the Holy Spirit, and you will simply outstrip everything they have in any college there ever was. You will leave them all behind, just as I have seen the sun leave the mist behind in San Francisco. You will leave what is as cold as ice and go into the sunshine.

God the Holy Spirit wants us to know the reality of this fullness of the Spirit so that we will neither be ignorant nor have mystic conceptions but will have a clear, unmistakable revelation of the entire mind of God for these days.

I implore you, beloved, in the name of Jesus, that you should see that you come right into all the mind of God. Jesus truly said, *"But you shall receive power when the Holy Spirit has come upon you"* (Acts 1:8 NKJV).

Thought for today: Jesus is all the time unfolding to every one of us the power of resurrection.

DAY 31

EQUIPPED WITH POWER

Seek out from among you seven men of good reputation,
full of the Holy Spirit and wisdom,
whom we may appoint over this business.
—Acts 6:3 (NKJV)

Scripture reading: Acts 6:1–7

During the time of the inauguration of the church, the disciples were pressured by many responsibilities. The practical things of life could not be attended to, and many were complaining concerning the neglect of their widows. Therefore, the disciples decided to choose seven men to do the work of caring for the needs of these widows—men who were "*full of the Holy Spirit.*" What a divine thought. No matter what kind of work was to be done, however menial it may have been, the person chosen had to be "*full of the Holy Spirit.*" The plan of the church was that everything, even everyday routines, must be sanctified to God, for the church had to be a Holy Spirit church. Beloved, God has never ordained anything less.

The heritage of the church is to be so equipped with power that God can lay His hand upon any member at any time to do His perfect will. There is no stopping point in the Spirit-filled life. We begin at the Cross, the place of disgrace, shame, and death, and that very death brings the power of resurrection life. Then, being filled with the Holy Spirit, we go on "*from glory to glory*" (2 Corinthians 3:18). Let us not forget that possessing the baptism in the Holy Spirit means that there must be an ever-increasing holiness. People know when the tide is flowing; they also know when it is ebbing. How the church needs divine anointing! It needs to see God's presence and power so evidenced that the world will recognize it.

Thought for today: When we please God in our daily service, we will always find that everyone who is faithful in the little things, God will make ruler over much. (See Matthew 25:21.)

DAY 32

ABOVE THE ORDINARY

They chose Stephen, a man full of faith and the Holy Spirit.
—Acts 6:5 (NKJV)

Scripture reading: Acts 6:8–15; 7:55–60

God has privileged us in Christ Jesus to live above the ordinary human plane of life. Those who want to be ordinary and live on a lower plane can do so, but as for me, I will not. The same anointing, the same zeal, the same Holy Spirit power is at our command as it was at the command of Stephen and the apostles. We have the same God that Abraham and Elijah had, and we do not need to lag behind in receiving any gift or grace. We may not possess all the gifts as abiding gifts, but as we are full of the Holy Spirit and divine anointing, it is possible, when there is a need, for God to make evident every gift of the Spirit through us as He may choose.

Stephen, an ordinary man, became extraordinary under the Holy Spirit's anointing until, in many ways, he stands supreme among the apostles. *"And Stephen, full of faith and power, did great wonders and miracles among the people"* (Acts 6:8). As we go deeper in God, He enlarges our capacity for understanding and places before us a wide-open door. It is not surprising that this man chosen to serve tables was later called to a higher plane.

You may ask, "What do you mean? Did he stop taking care of his responsibilities?" No, but he was lost in the power of God. He lost sight of everything in the natural and steadfastly fixed his gaze on Jesus, *"the author and finisher of our faith"* (Hebrews 12:2), until he was transformed into a shining light in the kingdom of God. May we be awakened to believe His Word and to understand the mind of the Spirit, for there is an inner place of purity where we can see God. Stephen was an ordinary person, but he was in the place where God could move him so that he, in turn, could affect those around him. He began in a humble place and ended in a blaze of glory. Dare to believe Christ.

Thought for today: Chosen for menial service, Stephen became mighty for God.

DAY 33

THE MASTER'S TOUCH

Do all things without murmurings and disputings:
that you may be blameless and harmless, the sons of God,
without rebuke, in the midst of a crooked and perverse nation,
among whom you shine as lights in the world.
—Philippians 2:14–15

Scripture reading: James 1:16–27

I see many remarkable things in the life of Stephen. One thing moves me, and that is the truth that I must live by the power of the Spirit at all costs. God wants us to be like Stephen: *"full of faith and the Holy Spirit"* (Acts 6:5 NKJV). You can never be the same again after you have received this wonderful baptism in the Holy Spirit. It is important that we should be full of wisdom and faith day by day and full of the Holy Spirit, acting by the power of the Holy Spirit. God has set us here in the last days, these days of apostasy, and wants us to be burning and shining lights in the midst of an indecent generation. God is longing for us to come into such a fruitful position as the children of God, with the marks of heaven upon us and with His divinity bursting through our humanity, that He can express Himself through our lips of clay. He can take clay lips and weak humanity and make an oracle for Himself of such things. He can take frail human nature and by His divine power make our bodies suitable to be His holy temple, washing our hearts whiter than snow.

Our Lord Jesus says, *"All power is given to Me in heaven and in earth"* (Matthew 28:18). He longs that we would be filled with faith and with the Holy Spirit, and He declares to us, *"He that believes on Me, the works that I do shall he do also; and greater works than these shall he do; because I go to My Father"* (John 14:12). He has gone to the Father. He is in the place of power, and He exercises His power not only in heaven but also on earth, for He has all power on earth as well as in heaven. Hallelujah! What an open door to us if we will only believe Him!

The disciples were men after our standard as far as the flesh goes. God sent them forth, joined to the Lord and identified with Him. How diverse Peter, John, and Thomas were! Impulsive Peter was always ready to go forth without a stop. John, the beloved, leaned on the Master's breast. (See John 21:20.) Thomas had a hard nature and defiant spirit: *"Except I…put my finger into the print of the nails, and thrust my hand into His side, I will not believe"* (John 20:25). What strange flesh! How peculiar they were! But the Master could mold them. There was no touch like His.

Under His touch, even stony-hearted Thomas believed. Oh, my God, how You have had to manage some of us! Have we not been strange and very peculiar? But when God's hand comes upon us, He can speak to us in such a way; He can give us a word or a look, and we are broken. Has He spoken to you? I thank God for His speaking. Behind all of His dealings, we see the love of God for us. He sees our bitter tears and our weeping night after night. There is none like Him. He knows; He forgives. We cannot forgive ourselves; we oftentimes would give the world to forget, but we cannot. The devil won't let us forget. But God has forgiven and forgotten. Do you believe self or the devil or God? Which are you going to believe? Believe God. I know the past is under the blood of Christ and that God has forgiven and forgotten, for when He forgives, He forgets. Praise the Lord! Hallelujah! We are baptized to believe and to receive.

Thought for today: It is not what we are that counts but what we can be as He disciplines, chastens, and transforms us by His all-skillful hands.

DAY 34

FULL OF FAITH AND POWER

Stephen, full of faith and power, did great wonders and miracles.
—Acts 6:8

Scripture reading: Luke 4:1–19

In the early days of the church, all who did the work of serving had to be full of the Holy Spirit. The greatest qualification for ministry is to be filled with the Spirit.

Stephen was a man *"full of faith and the Holy Spirit"* (Acts 6:5 NKJV). God so manifested Himself in Stephen's body that he became an epistle of truth, known and read by all. He was full of faith! Such men never talk doubtfully. You never hear them say, "I wish it could be so," or "If it is God's will." They have no *ifs*; they know. You never hear them say, "Well, it is not always so." They say, "It is sure to be." They laugh at impossibilities and cry, "It will be done!" They shout while the walls are up and when they come down. God has this faith for us in Christ. We must be careful that no unbelief and no wavering are found in us.

"Stephen, full of faith and power, did great wonders and miracles among the people" (Acts 6:8). The Holy Spirit could do mighty things through him because he believed God, and God is with the man who dares to believe His Word. All things were possible because of the Holy Spirit's position in Stephen's body. Because Stephen was full of the Holy Spirit, God could fulfill His purposes through him. When a child of God is filled with the Holy Spirit, the Spirit *"makes intercession for the saints according to the will of God"* (Romans 8:27). He fills us with longings and desires until we are in a place of fervency like a glowing fire. When we do not know what to do, the Holy Spirit begins to work. When the Holy Spirit has liberty in the body, He conveys all prayers into the presence of God. Such prayers are

always heard. Such praying is always answered; it is never bare of result. When we are praying in the Holy Spirit, faith is evident, and as a result the power of God can be manifested in our midst.

When some of the various synagogues arose to dispute with Stephen, "*they were not able to resist the wisdom and the Spirit by which he spoke*" (Acts 6:10). When we are filled with the Holy Spirit, we will have wisdom.

Thought for today: A man full of faith hopes against hope.

DAY 35

FAITH AND REMEMBRANCE

The word preached did not profit them,
not being mixed with faith in them that heard it.
—Hebrews 4:2

Scripture reading: Psalm 119:41–50; Luke 22:15–20

The words of Jesus are life—never think they are less. If you believe them, you will feel quickened. The Word is powerful; it is full of faith. The Word of God is vital. Faith is established and made manifest as we hear the Word. Beloved, read the Word of God in quietude, and read it out loud, for *"he that hears My word"* (John 5:24), to him it gives life.

Listen to these words from Scripture: *"With desire I have desired to eat this passover with you before I suffer"* (Luke 22:15); *"The hour is come; behold, the Son of Man is betrayed into the hands of sinners"* (Mark 14:41). From the beginning of time, there has never been an hour like this. These words were among the greatest that Jesus ever spoke: *"The hour is come."*

Time was finished and eternity had begun for every soul that was covered with the blood. Until that hour, all people lived only to die, but the moment the sacrifice was made, it was not the end but only the beginning. The soul, covered with the blood, has moved from a natural to an eternal union with the Lord. Instead of death will be the fullness of life divine.

While I was in Jerusalem, I preached many weeks outside the Damascus Gate, and God mightily blessed my ministry. It is wonderful to be in the place where God can use you. As I was leaving Jerusalem, some Jews who had heard me preach wanted to travel with me and stay at the same hotel where I was staying. When we were sitting around the table eating, they said, "What we cannot understand is that when you preach, we feel such power. You move us. There is something about it; we cannot help but feel that you have something different from what we have been used to hearing. What is it?"

I replied that it was because I preached Jesus in the power of the Holy Spirit, for He was the Messiah, and He causes a child of His to live in the reality of a clear knowledge of Himself so that others know and feel His power. It is this knowledge that the church today needs so much.

Do not be satisfied with anything less than the knowledge of a real change in your nature, the knowledge of the indwelling presence and power of the Holy Spirit. Do not be satisfied with a life that is not wholly swallowed up in God.

There are many books written about the Word, and we love clear, definite teaching on it. But go to the Book, and listen to what the Master says. You will lay a sure foundation that cannot be moved, for we are born again by the incorruptible Word of God. (See 1 Peter 1:23.) We need the simplicity, the rest of faith, that brings us to the place where we are steadfast and immovable. How wonderful the living Word of God is!

Can you not see that the Master was so interested in you that He would despise the shame of the cross? (See Hebrews 12:2.) The judgment hall was nothing to Him; all the rebukes and scorn could not take from Him the joy of saving you and me. His sacrificial love and joy caused Him to say, "I consider nothing too vile to endure on behalf of Wigglesworth; I count nothing too horrid to bear for Brown; My soul is on the wing to save the world!" How beautiful this is! How it should thrill us! He knew that death was represented in that sacred cup, yet He joyfully said, *"With desire I have desired to eat this passover with you before I suffer"* (Luke 22:15). Take the bread, drink of the cup, and as often as you take it, remember. (See 1 Corinthians 11:24–25.) In other words, take the memory of what it means home with you; think on it, and analyze its meaning.

As we come to the time of the breaking of bread, the thought should be, "How should I partake of it?" We should be able to say, "Lord, I desire to eat it to please You, for I want my whole life to be for You!" As the stream of the new life begins to flow through your being, allow yourself to be immersed and carried on until your life becomes a ceaseless flow of the river of life. Then it will be *"not I, but Christ lives in me"* (Galatians 2:20). Get ready for the breaking of bread and for partaking of the wine, and in doing so, remember Him.

Thought for today: We are no better than our faith.

DAY 36

DIVINE AUTHORITY

Put on the whole armor of God, that you may be able to stand against the wiles of the devil.
—Ephesians 6:11

Scripture reading: Ephesians 6:10–18

I am more and more convinced every day I live that very few who are saved by the grace of God have a right conception of how great their authority is over darkness, demons, death, and every power of the Enemy. It is a real joy when we realize our inheritance.

I was speaking like this one day, and someone said, "I have never heard anything like this before. How many months did it take you to think up that sermon?"

I said, "My brother, God pressed my wife from time to time to get me to preach, and I promised her I would preach. I used to labor hard for a week to think something up, then give out the text and sit down and say, 'I am done.' Oh, brother, I have given up thinking things up. They all come down. And the sermons that come down, stop down, then go back, because the Word of God says His Word will not return to Him void. (See Isaiah 55:11.) If you get anything up in your own power, it will not stay up very long; when it goes down, it will take you down with it."

The sons of God are made manifest in this present earth to destroy the power of the devil. To be saved by the power of God is to be brought from the realm of the ordinary into the extraordinary, from the natural into the divine.

Do you remember the day when the Lord laid His hands on you? You say, "I could not do anything except praise the Lord." Well, that was only the beginning. Where are you today? The divine plan is that you increase until you receive the measureless fullness of God. You do not have to say, "I tell you it was wonderful when I was baptized with the Holy Spirit." If you have to look back to the past to make me know you are baptized, then you are backslidden.

If the beginning was good, it ought to be better day by day, until everybody is fully convinced that you are filled with the might of God in the Spirit, *"filled with all the fullness of God"* (Ephesians 3:19). *"Be not drunk with wine, wherein is excess; but be filled with the Spirit"* (Ephesians 5:18). I don't want anything other than being full and fuller and fuller, until I am overflowing like a great big vat. Do you realize that if you have been created anew and born again by the Word of God that there is within you the word of power and the same light and life that the Son of God Himself had?

God wants to flow through you with measureless power of divine utterance and grace until your whole body is a flame of fire. So many people have been baptized with the Holy Spirit; there was a movement, but they have become monuments, and you cannot move them. God, wake us out of sleep lest we should become indifferent to the glorious truth and the breath of Your almighty power. We must be the light and salt of the earth (see Matthew 5:13–14), with the whole armor of God upon us (see Ephesians 6:11). It would be a serious thing if the enemies were about and we had to go back and get our shoes. It would be a serious thing if we had on no breastplate.

How can we be furnished with the armor? Take it by faith. Jump in, stop in, and never come out, for this is a baptism to be lost in, where you only know one thing, and that is the desire of God at all times. The baptism in the Spirit should be an ever increasing endowment of power, an ever increasing enlargement of grace. Oh, Father, grant us a real look into the glorious liberty You have designed for the children of God, who are delivered from this present world, separated, sanctified, and made suitable for Your use, whom You have designed to be filled with all Your fullness.

Thought for today: God intends each soul in Pentecost to be a live wire—not a monument, but a movement.

DAY 37

THE PURPOSE OF THE POWER

And they were all filled with the Holy Spirit and began to speak with other tongues, as the Spirit gave them utterance.
—Acts 2:4 (NKJV)

Scripture reading: Acts 1:4–14; 2:1–4

Before Jesus went to heaven, He told His disciples that they would receive the power of the Holy Spirit. (See Acts 1:8.) Thus, through them, His gracious ministry would continue. This power of the Holy Spirit was not only for a few apostles but even for those who were afar off (see Acts 2:39), even for us way down in this century. Some ask, "But wasn't this power just for the privileged few in the first century?" No. Read the Master's Great Commission as recorded in Mark 16:15–18, and you will see it is for those who believe.

After I received the baptism in the Holy Spirit, I sought the mind of the Lord as to why I had been baptized. One day I came home from work and went into the house. My wife asked me, "Which way did you come in?" I told her that I had come in the back door. She said, "There is a woman upstairs who has brought an eighty-year-old man to be prayed for. He is raving, and a great crowd has gathered outside the front door, ringing the doorbell and wanting to know what is going on in the house." The Lord quietly whispered, "This is what I baptized you for."

I carefully opened the door of the room where the man was, desiring to be obedient to what my Lord would say to me. The man was crying and shouting in distress, "I am lost! I am lost! I have committed the unpardonable sin. I am lost! I am lost!" My wife asked, "Smith, what should we do?" The Spirit of the Lord moved me to cry out, "Come out, you lying spirit." In a moment the evil spirit went, and the man was free. God gives deliverance to the captives. And the Lord said again to me, "This is what I baptized you for." There is a place where God, through the power of the Holy Spirit, reigns supreme in our lives. The Spirit reveals, unfolds, and takes of the things of Christ and shows them to us. (See John 16:14.)

Thought for today: The Holy Spirit prepares us to be more than a match for satanic forces.

DAY 38

HOW TO OBTAIN SPIRITUAL POWER

How can you believe, which receive honor one of another, and seek not the honor that comes from God only?
—John 5:44

Scripture reading: Matthew 16:13–23

In Peter's life, we see evidences of the spiritual power that he had attained, but we see also the natural power working. Jesus saw that He must suffer if He would reach the spiritual life that God intended Him to reach, so Jesus said, "I must go forward. Your words, Peter, are an offense to Me." (See Matthew 16:23.) If you to seek to save yourself, it is an offense to God. God has been impressing on me more and more that if at any time I were to seek man's favor or earthly power, I would lose favor with God and could not have faith.

God is speaking to us, every one of us, trying to get us to leave the shoreline. There is only one place where we can have the mind and will of God; it is alone with God. If we look to anybody else, we cannot get it. If we seek to save ourselves, we will never reach the place where we will be able to bind and loose. (See Matthew 16:19.) There is a close companionship between you and Jesus that nobody knows about, where every day you have to choose or refuse.

It is in the narrow way that you get the power to bind and the power to loose. I know that Jesus was separated from His own family and friends. He was deprived of the luxuries of life. It seems to me that God wants to get every one of us separated to Himself in this holy war, and we are not going to have faith if we do not give ourselves wholly to Him. Beloved, it is in these last days that I cannot have the power I want to have unless, as a sheep, I am willing to shear myself. The way is narrow. (See Matthew 7:13–14.)

Beloved, you will not be able to bind and loose if you have sin in you. There is not one person who is able to deal with the sins of others if he is not free himself. *"He breathed on them, and said to them, 'Receive the Holy Spirit'"* (John 20:22 NKJV). Jesus knew the Holy Spirit would give them both a revelation of themselves and a revelation of God. He must reveal to you your depravity.

Do you believe that the Father in heaven would make you a judge over a kingdom if there were anything crooked in you? Do you believe you will be able to bind unless you are free yourself? But everyone who has this living Christ within him has the power that will put to death all sin.

With Jesus's last words on earth, He gave the disciples a commission. (See Mark 16:15–18.) The need for discipleship has never ceased. Some churches are weak today because Christ the Rock is not abiding in them in the manifestations of the power of God. This is not because it is a special gift—this power to bind and loose—but it is contingent on whether you have the rock foundation in you. In the name of Jesus, you will loose, and in the name of Jesus, you will bind. If He is in you, you ought to bring forth evidences of that power.

One can see that Peter had great sympathy, and he did not want Jesus to be crucified. It was perfectly natural for Peter to say what he did, but Jesus said, *"Get you behind Me"* (Matthew 16:23). He knew He must not be turned aside by any human sympathy. The only way we can retain our humility is to stay on this narrow line and say, "Get behind me, Satan."

Beloved, we are now living in the experience of the fact that Jesus is the Rock. I am glad, for we are within reach of wonderful possibilities because of the Rock. Take a stand on the fact that the Rock cannot be overthrown.

Thought for today: If you try to go the easy way, you cannot be Jesus's disciple.

DAY 39

HOW TO BRING CONVICTION OF SIN

When He [the Holy Spirit] *is come, He will reprove the world of sin, and of righteousness, and of judgment.*
—John 16:8

Scripture reading: Ephesians 5:8–21

Do you believe that you can be so filled with the Spirit that a person who is not living right can be judged and convicted by your presence? As we go on in the life of the Spirit, it will be said of us that a vile person is convicted in our presence. Jesus lived in this realm and moved in it, and His life was a constant reproof to the wickedness around Him. "But He was the Son of God," you say. God, through Him, has brought us into the place of sonship, and I believe that if the Holy Spirit has a chance at us, He can make something of us and bring us to the same place.

I don't want to boast. If I glory in anything, it is only in the Lord (see 1 Corinthians 1:31), who has been so gracious to me, but I remember a wonderful time of conviction. I stepped out of a railway coach to wash my hands. I had a season of prayer, and the Lord just filled me to overflowing with His love. I was going to a convention in Ireland, and I could not get there fast enough. As I returned to my seat, I believe that the Spirit of the Lord was so heavy upon me that my face must have shone. (When the Spirit transforms a man's very countenance, he cannot tell this on his own.) There were two ministers sitting together, and as I got into the coach again, one of them cried out, "You convict me of sin." Within three minutes everyone in the coach was crying to God for salvation. This has happened many times in my life. It is the ministry of the Spirit that Paul spoke of. This filling of the Spirit will make your life effective, so that even the people in the stores where you shop will want to leave your presence because they are brought under conviction.

We must move away from everything that pertains to the letter. All that we do must be done under the anointing of the Spirit. Our problem has been that we have been living in the letter. Believe what the Holy Spirit said through Paul—that this entire *"ministration of condemnation"* (2 Corinthians 3:9) that has hindered your liberty in Christ is done away with. The law has been done away with. As far as you are concerned, that old order of things is forever done away with, and the Spirit of God has brought in a new life of purity and love. In the life in the Spirit, the old allurements have lost their power. The devil will meet you at every turn, but the Spirit of God will always *"lift up a standard against him"* (Isaiah 59:19).

If God had His way, we would be like torches, purifying the very atmosphere wherever we go, moving back the forces of wickedness.

What do I mean when I say that the law has been done away with? Do I mean that you will be disloyal? No, you will be more than loyal. Will you grumble when you are treated badly? No, you will turn the other cheek. (See Matthew 5:39.) You will always respond this way when God lives in you. Leave yourself in God's hands. Enter into His rest. *"For he that is entered into His rest, he also has ceased from his own works, as God did from His"* (Hebrews 4:10). Oh, this is a lovely rest! The whole life is a Sabbath. This is the only life that can glorify God. It is a life of joy, and every day is a day of heaven on earth.

Thought for today: The Holy Spirit takes it for granted that you are finished with all the things of the old life when you become a new creation in Christ.

DAY 40

OUR JOINT INHERITANCE

This grace given, that I should preach among the Gentiles the unsearchable riches of Christ.
—Ephesians 3:8

Scripture reading: Galatians 3:7–29

The fullness of the expression of the Holy Spirit today is giving us a glimpse into what has been provided by the Father. We know that in the old Israel, from Abraham right down, God had a special relationship with His chosen people.

But the Gentiles had no right to it. The Master said to the Syrophenician woman, "Shall I take the bread of the children and give it to dogs?" (See Mark 7:27.) Did Jesus mean that the Gentiles were dogs? No, He meant that the whole race of the Gentiles knew that they were far below the standard and the order of those people who belonged to the royal stock of Israel. The Samaritans all felt it.

"But isn't it possible for the dogs to have some crumbs?" was the woman's question. (See v. 28.) God has something better than crumbs. He has made the Gentiles of the same body, the same heirs as His chosen people. He has put no difference between them and us, but He has included us in the promises for all who are forgiven by the blood of Christ. Paul spoke about it, knowing that *"if you be Christ's, then are you Abraham's seed, and heirs according to the promise"* (Galatians 3:29).

Thank God! God so manifests His power that He has brought us into oneness, and we know we are sharing in the glory. We are sharing in the knowledge that we belong to the aristocracy of the church of God.

It is wonderful to know that I am in the body. It is wonderful to know that the apostles and prophets and all those who have passed down the years, holding aloft the torch, going on from victory to victory, all will be in the body. But how wonderful if we may be in the body so that we might be chosen out of the body to be the bride! It will be according as you are yielded to the *"effectual working of His power"* (Ephesians 3:7).

Thought for today: God has met the needs of all nations, of all ranks, of all conditions.

DAY 41

YOUR PART IN THE BODY

That the Gentiles should be fellow-heirs, and of the same body, and partakers of His promise in Christ by the gospel.
—Ephesians 3:6

Scripture reading: 1 Corinthians 12:12–27

I want you to see your place in the body of Christ. There is no greater language than this about the Lord, that all fullness dwells in Him. (See Colossians 1:19.) Christ is to be manifested fully in humanity.

Do not be afraid of claiming your right. It is not a measure that you have to reach. Remember, John saw Him, and he said that he had a measure that could not be measured. Christ is coming to us in a measureless measure. Human calculation cannot fathom it.

The church is rising in all her vision and destroying the powers of darkness, ruling among the powers of wickedness, and transforming darkness to light by the power of the new creation in us. The church is doing all this so that we might know the power that is working in us by the resurrection of the life of Christ.

So we are enriched with all enrichment; we are endued with all beatitudes; we are covered with all graces; and now we are coming into all the mysteries so that the gifts of the Spirit may be manifested in us.

The revelation of Paul, which never from the foundation of the world had been revealed, is that the Son of God, the very embodiment of the nature of the Most High, the very incarnation of His presence and power, could fill a human vessel to its utmost capacity, until His very nature will sweep through by the power of God.

You cannot enter into this life without being enlarged, abounding, and superabundant. Everything in God is enlargement. God never wants a child of His in the world to be measured. All the riches of God are infinite and boundless. There is no such thing as measuring them. If ever you measure God, you will be thin and little and dwarfed. You cannot measure. You have an exhaustless place.

God's Son is in you with all the power of development, until you are so enriched by this divine grace that you live in the world knowing that God is transforming you from grace to grace, from victory to victory.

The Spirit in you has no other foundation than from glory unto glory. Paul was so enlarged in the Spirit in this third chapter of Ephesians that his language failed to express the glory of Christ Jesus. And then, when he failed to go on in his language, he bowed his knees unto the Father. Oh, this is supreme! This is beyond all that could be! When language failed, when prophecy had no more room, it seems that he came to a place where he got down on his knees. Then we hear by the power of the Spirit language beyond all Paul could ever say: *"For this cause I bow my knees to the Father of our Lord Jesus Christ, of whom the whole family in heaven and earth is named"* (Ephesians 3:14–15).

Paul realized that he was joining earth and heaven together. They are one, thank God! There is nothing between us and heaven. Gravity may hold us, but all in heaven and in earth are joined under one blood, with no division or separation. *"To be absent from the body, and to be present with the Lord"* (2 Corinthians 5:8).

Thought for today: You might measure your land, you might measure your harvest, but you cannot measure the purposes of the Spirit life: they are boundless; they are infinite.

DAY 42

SUPERNATURAL FULLNESS

The thief comes not, but for to steal, and to kill, and to destroy:
I am come that they might have life,
and that they might have it more abundantly.
—John 10:10

Scripture reading: Romans 8:1–17

If I cannot make a person who is suffering from disease righteously indignant against that condition, I cannot help him. If I can make a sufferer know that suffering, disease, and all these things are the workings of the devil, I can help him.

If you can see that the devil is after you, to kill you for all he is worth, believe that Christ is enthroned in your heart to destroy the very principles of the devil in every way. Have the reality of this; build upon it by perfect soundness until you are in the place of perfect bliss, for to know Christ is perfect bliss. Be so built in Him that you are not afraid of evil. You must have a fullness that presses out beyond; you must have a life that is full of divine power; you must have a mind that is perfectly in Christ; you must cease to be natural and begin to be supernatural.

Are you ready to be so changed by God that you will never have this human fear anymore? Remember that *"perfect love casts out fear"* (1 John 4:18).

Step into the full tide of the life of the manifestation of God. Your new nature has no corruption in it. Eternal life is not just during your lifetime; it is forever. You are regenerated by the power of the Word of God, and it is in you as an incorruptible force, taking you on from victory to victory until death itself can be overcome, until sin has no authority, until disease could not be in the body. This is a living fact by the Word of God.

Right in this present moment, there is *"no condemnation"* (Romans 8:1). This law of the Spirit of life is a law in the body; it is a law of eternity; it is a law of God, a new law. It is not the law of the Ten Commandments, but a law of life in the body, changing you until there is no sin power, no disease power, and no death power.

You who desire to go a thousand miles through faith, beyond what you have ever gone before, leap into it. Believe that the blood of Christ makes you clean; believe that you have come into resurrection life. Believe it!

Trying is an effort, whereas believing is a fact. Don't join the Endeavor Society, but come into the Faith Society, and you will leap into the promises of God, which are *"Yea"* and *"Amen"* (2 Corinthians 1:20) to all who believe.

Don't look down your nose and murmur anymore. Have a rejoicing spirit; get the praise of God in your heart; go forth from victory to victory; rise in faith, and believe it. You must not live in yourself; you must live in Christ. *"Set your affection on things above"* (Colossians 3:2), and keep your whole spirit alive in God. Let your inheritance be so full of divine life that you live above the world and all its thoughts and cares.

Thought for today: God is on His throne and can take you a thousand miles in a moment. Have faith to jump into His supernatural plan.

DAY 43

WHAT IS INSIDE WILL COME OUT

As in water face answers to face, so the heart of man to man.
—Proverbs 27:19

Scripture reading: Matthew 15:1–20

We praise God that our glorious Jesus is the risen Christ. Those of us who have tasted the power of the indwelling Spirit know something about how the hearts of those two disciples burned as they walked to Emmaus with the risen Lord as their companion. (See Luke 24:13–32.)

Note the words of Acts 4:31: *"And when they had prayed, the place was shaken where they were assembled together."* There are many churches where they never pray the kind of prayer that you read of here. A church that does not know how to pray and to shout will never be shaken. If you live in a place like that, you might as well write over the threshold: "Ichabod"—*"The glory is departed from Israel"* (1 Samuel 4:21). It is only when men have learned the secret of prayer, power, and praise that God comes forth. Some people say, "Well, I praise God inwardly," but if your heart is full of praise, you will have to let the praise come out.

The inner working of the power of God must come first. It is He who changes the heart and transforms the life. Before there is any real outward evidence, there must be the inflow of divine life. Sometimes I say to people, "You weren't at the meeting the other night." They reply, "Oh yes, I was there in spirit." I say to them, "Well, next time come with your body also. We don't want a lot of spirits here and no bodies. We want you to come and get filled with God." When all the people come and pray and praise as did these early disciples, there will be something happening. People who come will catch fire, and they will want to come again. But they will have no use for a place where everything has become formal, dry, and dead.

The power of Pentecost came in order to loose men. God wants us to be free. Men and women are tired of imitations; they want reality; they want to see people who have the living Christ within, who are filled with Holy Spirit power.

Thought for today: The shout cannot come out unless it is within.

DAY 44

FAITH LIKE ABRAHAM

To them that have obtained like precious faith with us through the righteousness of God and our Savior Jesus Christ.
—2 Peter 1:1

Scripture reading: John 6:22–51

As we are filled with the Holy Spirit, God purposes that like our Lord, we should love righteousness and hate lawlessness. There is a place for us in Christ Jesus where we are no longer under condemnation but where the heavens are always open to us. God has a realm of divine life opening up to us where there are boundless possibilities, limitless power, and untold resources. We have victory over all the power of the devil. As we are filled with the desire to press on into this life of true holiness, desiring only the glory of God, nothing can hinder our true advancement.

Through faith, we realize that we have a blessed and glorious union with our risen Lord. When He was on earth, Jesus told us, *"I am in the Father, and the Father in Me"* (John 14:11). *"The Father that dwells in Me, He does the works"* (v. 10). He prayed to His Father not only for His disciples but also for those who would believe on Him through their testimonies: *"That they all may be one; as You, Father, are in Me, and I in You, that they also may be one in Us: that the world may believe that You have sent Me"* (John 17:21). What an inheritance is ours when the very nature, the very righteousness, the very power of the Father and the Son are made real in us. This is God's purpose, and as we take hold of the purpose by faith, we will always be conscious that *"greater is He that is in you, than he that is in the world"* (1 John 4:4). The purpose of all Scripture is to move us to this wonderful and blessed elevation of faith where our constant experience is the manifestation of God's life and power through us.

Peter went on writing to those who had obtained *"like precious faith,"* saying, *"Grace and peace be multiplied to you through the knowledge of God, and of Jesus our Lord"* (2 Peter 1:2). We can have the multiplication of this grace and peace only as we live in the realm of faith. Abraham reached the place where he became *"the Friend of God"* because he *"believed God"* (James 2:23). He *"believed God, and it was imputed to him for righteousness"* (v. 23). Righteousness was credited to him on no other ground than that he *"believed God."* Can this be true of anybody else? Yes, it can be true for every person in the whole wide world who is saved and is blessed along with faithful Abraham.

Some people are anxious because, when they are prayed for, the thing that they are expecting does not happen right then. They say they believe, but you can see that they are really in turmoil from their unbelief. Abraham believed God. You can hear him saying to Sarah, "Sarah, there is no life in you, and there is nothing in me; but God has promised us a son, and I believe God." That kind of faith is a joy to our Father in heaven.

Thought for today: When we believe God, there is no telling where the blessings of our faith will end.

DAY 45

ASK LARGELY OF GOD

He that believes on Me, as the scripture has said, out of his belly shall flow rivers of living water.
—John 7:38

Scripture reading: John 7:37–8:12

I know that dry ground can be flooded. (See Isaiah 44:3.) May God prevent me from ever wanting anything less than a flood. Through the blood of Christ's atonement, we may have riches and riches. We need the warming atmosphere of the Spirit's power to bring us closer and closer until nothing but God can satisfy. Then we may have some idea of what God has left after we have taken all that we can. It is like a sparrow taking a drink of the ocean and then looking around and saying, "What a vast ocean! I could have taken a lot more if only I had room."

Sometimes you have things you can use, and you don't know it. You could be dying of thirst right in a river of plenty. There was once a boat in the mouth of the Amazon River. The people on board thought they were still in the ocean. They were dying of thirst, some of them nearly mad. They saw a ship and asked if they would give them some water. Someone on the ship replied, "Dip your bucket right over; you are in the mouth of the river." There are a number of people today in the middle of the great river of life, but they are dying of thirst because they do not dip down and take from the river. Dear friend, you may have the Word, but you need an awakened spirit. The Word is not alive until it is moved upon by the Spirit of God, and in the right sense, it becomes Spirit and Life when it is touched by His hand alone.

Beloved, *"there is a river, the streams whereof shall make glad the city of God, the holy place of the tabernacles of the Most High"* (Psalm 46:4). There is a stream of life that makes everything move. There is a touch of divine life and likeness through the Word of God that comes from nowhere else. We think of death as the absence of life, but there is a likeness of death in Christ, who is full of life.

There is no such thing as an end to God's beginnings. We must be in Christ; we must know Him. Life in Christ is not a touch; it is not a breath; it is the almighty God; it is a Person; it is the Holy One dwelling in the temple *"not made with hands"* (Hebrews 9:11). Oh, beloved, He touches, and it is done. He is the same God over all, *"rich to all that call upon Him"* (Romans 10:12). Pentecost is the last thing that God has to touch the earth with. If you do not receive the baptism of the Holy Spirit, you are living in a weak and impoverished condition, which is no good to you or anybody else. May God move us on to a place where there is no measure to this fullness that He wants to give us. God exalted Jesus and gave Him a name above every name. You notice that everything has been put under Him.

The tide is rolling in. Let us see to it today that we get right into the tide, for it will hold us. God's heart of love is the center of all things. Get your eyes off yourself; lift them up high, and see the Lord, for in Him, there *"is everlasting strength"* (Isaiah 26:4).

If you went to see a doctor, the more you told him about yourself, the more he would know. But when you come to Doctor Jesus, He knows all from the beginning, and He never prescribes the wrong medicine. Jesus sends His healing power and brings His restoring grace, so there is nothing to fear. The only thing that is wrong is your wrong conception of His redemption.

Thought for today: I will not settle for small things when I have such a big God.

DAY 46

TAKE AUTHORITY OVER SATAN

Get you behind Me, Satan.
—Luke 4:8

Scripture reading: Luke 4:1–13

Jesus was wounded so that He might be able to identify with your weaknesses. (See Hebrews 4:15.) He took your flesh and laid it upon the cross so that *"He might destroy him that had the power of death, that is, the devil; and deliver them who through fear of death were all their lifetime subject to bondage"* (Hebrews 2:14–15).

You will find that almost all the ailments that you experience come as a result of Satan, and they must be dealt with as satanic; they must be cast out. Do not listen to what Satan says to you, for the devil is a liar from the beginning. (See John 8:44.) If people would only listen to the truth of God, they would realize that every evil spirit is subject to them. They would find out that they are always in the place of triumph, and they would *"reign in life by One, Jesus Christ"* (Romans 5:17).

Never live in a place other than where God has called you, and He has called you from on high to live with Him. God has designed that everything will be subject to man. Through Christ, He has given you authority over all the power of the Enemy. He has worked out your eternal redemption.

I was finishing a meeting one day in Switzerland. When the meeting ended and we had ministered to all the sick, we went out to see some people. Two boys came to us and said that there was a blind man present at the meeting that afternoon. He had heard all the words of the preacher and said he was surprised that he had not been prayed for. They went on to say that this blind man had heard so much that he would not leave until he could see. I said, "This is positively unique. God will do something today for that man."

We got to the place. The blind man said he had never seen. He was born blind, but because of the Word preached in the afternoon, he was not going home until he could see. If ever I have joy, it is when I have a lot of people who will not be satisfied until they get all that they have come for. With great joy, I anointed him and laid hands on his eyes. Immediately, God restored his vision. It was very strange how the man reacted. There were some electric lights. First he counted them; then he counted us. Oh, the ecstatic pleasure that this man experienced every moment because of his sight! It made us all feel like weeping and dancing and shouting. Then he pulled out his watch and said that for years he had been feeling the raised figures on the watch in order to tell the time, but now he could look at it and tell us the time. Then, looking as if he had just awakened from some deep sleep or some long, strange dream, he realized that he had never seen the faces of his father and mother. He went to the door and rushed out. That night, he was the first person to arrive for the meeting. All the people knew him as the blind man, and I had to give him a long time to talk about his new sight.

I wonder how much you want to take with you today. You could not carry it if it were substance, but there is something about the grace, the power, and the blessings of God that can be carried, no matter how big they are. Oh, what a Savior! What a place we are in, by grace, that He may come in to commune with us. He is willing to say to every heart, *"Peace, be still"* (Mark 4:39), and to every weak body, *"Be strong"* (Deuteronomy 31:6). Are you going halfway, or are you going all the way to the end?

Thought for today: Do not be deceived by Satan, but believe God.

DAY 47

SANCTIFIED BY GOD

If any man hear My voice, and open the door, I will come in to him, and will sup with him, and he with Me.
—Revelation 3:20

Scripture reading: Colossians 1:9–23

Look at the tremendous power of God behind our inheritance. First, we are adopted; then we receive an inheritance; then we are made coheirs with Jesus. God touches our souls, making our whole bodies cry out for the living God.

Do you want God? Do you want fellowship in the Spirit? Do you want to walk with Him? Do you desire communion with Him? Everything else is no good. You want the association with God, and God says, *"I will come in to* [you], *and will sup with* [you], *and* [you] *with Me."* Hallelujah! We can attain spiritual maturity, fullness of Christ, a place where God becomes the perfect Father and the Holy Spirit has a rightful place now as never before.

The Holy Spirit breathes through us, enabling us to say, "You are my Father." Because you have been adopted, *"God has sent forth the Spirit of His Son into your hearts, crying, Abba, Father"* (Galatians 4:6). May God the Holy Spirit grant to us that richness of His pleasure, that unfolding of His will, that consciousness of His smile upon us. There is *"no condemnation"* (Romans 8:1). We find that *"the law of the Spirit of life"* makes us *"free from the law of sin and death"* (v. 2). Glory!

If we see the truth as clearly as God intends for us to see it, we will all be made so much richer, looking forward to the Blessed One who is coming again. Here we are, face-to-face with the facts. God has shown us different aspects of the Spirit. He has shown us the pavilion of splendor. He has revealed to us the power of the relationship of sonship. He has shown us that those who are God's children bear His image. They actively claim the rights of their adoption. They speak, and it is done. They bind the things that are loose, and loose the things that are bound. (See Matthew 16:19.) And the perfection of sonship is so evident that more and more people are becoming children of God.

Do you believe it? Let us see you act it. Beloved, God the Holy Spirit has a perfect plan to make us a movement. There is a difference between a movement and a monument. A movement is something that is always active. A monument is something that is erected on a corner and neither speaks nor moves, but there is a tremendous lot of humbug and nonsense to get it in place. It is silent and does nothing. A movement is where God comes into the very being of a person, making him active for God. He is God's property, God's mouthpiece, God's eyes, and God's hands. God will "*sanctify you wholly*" (1 Thessalonians 5:23).

The sanctification of the eyes, the hands, the mouth, the ears—to be so controlled by the Spirit who lives within us—is a wonderful place for God to bring us to. "*Beloved, now are we the sons of God, and it does not yet appear what we shall be*" (1 John 3:2). What a great thought: to be heirs, "*joint-heirs with Christ*" (Romans 8:17); to receive revelations and kindnesses from God; to have God dwell within man. The believer is filled, moved, and intensified until he takes wing. It would not take a trumpet to rouse him, for he is already on the wing, and he will land very soon. He would hear God's voice no matter how much noise surrounded him.

Everything that is going to help you, you have to make yours. He has stored it up already. You don't need a stepladder to get to it. It is ready to be handed to you when you become joined with Him. Beloved, it is impossible in our finite condition to estimate the lovingkindness or the measureless mind of God. When we come into like-mindedness with the Word, instead of looking at the Word, we begin to see what God has for us in the Word. Our prayer will be,

Me with a quenchless thirst inspire,
A longing, infinite desire
Fill my craving heart.

Less than Thyself You do not give,
Thy might within me now to live.
Come, all Thou hast.

God, please come and make it impossible for me to ever be satisfied but to always have an unquenchable desire for You, the living God. Then I will not be overtaken. Then I will be ready. Then I will have shining eyes, filled with delight as they look at the Master.

Thought for today: Will you shiver like someone hesitating on the edge of a pool? Or will you take a plunge into omnipotence and find the waters are not as cold as people told you?

DAY 48

THE SON OF GOD REVEALED

Herein is our love made perfect, that we may have boldness in the day of judgment: because as He is, so are we in this world.
—1 John 4:17

Scripture reading: Hebrews 2

You ask, "Can we see the Master?" Here, look at Him. His Word is Spirit and life-giving. This is the breath, the Word of Jesus. Through the Holy Spirit, men have written and spoken. Here is the life. Here is the witness. Here is the truth. Here is the Son of God *"revealed from faith to faith"* (Romans 1:17), from heart to heart, from vision to vision, until we all come into perfect unity of fellowship into the fullness of Christ.

There it is, beloved. Look! *"Now are we the sons of God"* (1 John 3:2). If you are there, we can take a step further. But if you are not there, you may hear but not cross over. There is something about the Word of God that benefits the hearer who has faith, but if the hearer does not have faith, it will not profit him.

The future is what you are today, not what you are going to be tomorrow. This is the day when God makes the future possible. When God reveals something to you today, tomorrow is filled with a further illumination of God's possibility for you.

Do you dare to come into the place of omnipotence, of wonderment? Do you dare to say to God, "I am ready for all that You have for me"? It will mean living a pure and holy life. It will mean living a sanctified, separate life. It will mean your heart is so perfect and your prospects are so divinely separated that you say to the world, "Goodbye."

The second chapter of Hebrews describes the mighty, glorified position for the children of God. God wants me to announce it to every heart, like a great trumpet call. The plan is to bring you to glory as a child clothed with the power of the gifts, graces, ministries, and operations. You are to be clothed with the majesty of heaven. This is like heaven to me. My very body is filled with thoughts of heaven.

Seeing that these things are so, what kind of people should we be? (See 2 Peter 3:11.) We should be keeping our eyes upon Him so that we may be ready for the rapture. Oh, brothers and sisters, what immense pleasure God has for us! There is no limit to the sober-mindedness God is bringing us to so that we may be able to understand all that God has planned for us. Oh, that we may look not on the things that are, but with eyes of purity see only the invisible Son. Having our whole bodies illuminated by the power of the Holy Spirit, we grow in grace, in faith, and in Christlikeness until there is no difference between us and Him.

Are you prepared to go all the way? Are you willing for your heart to have only one attraction? Are you willing to have only one Love? Are you willing for Him to become your perfect Bridegroom?

The more bridelike we are, the more we love to hear the Bridegroom's voice; the less bridelike we are, the less we long for His Word. If you cannot rest without it, if it becomes your food day and night, if you eat and drink of it, His life will be in you, and when He appears, you will go with Him. Help us, Jesus!

How many of you are prepared to reveal yourselves before the King? Are you prepared to yield to His call, yield to His will, yield to His desires? How many are going to say, "At all costs I will go through!" Who says so? Who means it? Are you determined? Is your soul on the wing? Make a full consecration to God right now. It is between you and God. You are going now to enter the presence of God.

Thought for today: Come clean with everything in the presence of God!

DAY 49

THE HOLY SPIRIT—OUR COMFORTER

Who comforts us in all our tribulation, that we may be able to comfort them which are in any trouble, by the comfort wherewith we ourselves are comforted of God.
—2 Corinthians 1:4

Scripture reading: 2 Corinthians 1:3–11

We need a revelation of a greater power, an abiding presence sustaining and comforting us in the hour of trial, ready at a moment's notice, an inbreathing of God in the human life. What more do we need in these last days when perilous times are upon us than to be filled, saturated, baptized with the Holy Spirit? Baptized. Baptized into Him, never to come out. How comforting! Exhilarating! Joyful! May it please the Lord to establish us in this state of grace. May we know nothing among men except Jesus Christ and Him crucified. (See 1 Corinthains 2:2.) May we be clothed with His Spirit—nothing outside of the blessed Holy Spirit. This, beloved, is God's ideal for us. Are we here in this experience?

Where He may lead me I will go,
For I have learned to trust Him so,
And I remember it was for me,
That He was slain on Calvary.

God has chosen me to go through certain experiences to profit others. In all ages, God has had His witnesses, and He is teaching, chastening, correcting, and moving me just up to the point that I am able to bear it, in order to meet a needy soul who would otherwise go down without such comfort. All the chastening and the hardship is because we are able to bear it. No, we are not able, but we yield to Another—even the Holy Spirit. We are strengthened so that we may endure and so that we may comfort others *"by the comfort wherewith we ourselves are comforted of God."*

Why do we need brokenness and travail? The reason can be found in the book of Psalms: *"Before I was afflicted I went astray: but now have I kept Your word"* (Psalm 119:67).

Thought for today: The God in you will not fail if you believe the Word of God.

DAY 50

AFLAME FOR GOD

Who makes His angels spirits, and His ministers a flame of fire.
—Hebrews 1:7

Scripture reading: Hebrews 1

God's ministers are to be flames of fire! It seems to me that no man with a vision, especially a vision by the Spirit's power, can read that wonderful verse without being kindled to such a flame of fire for his Lord that it seems as if it would burn up everything that would interfere with his progress.

A flame of fire! It is a perpetual fire; a constant fire; a continual burning; a holy, inward flame—which is exactly what God's Son was in the world. God has nothing less for us than to be flames! It seems to me that if Pentecost is to rise and be effective, we must have a living faith so that Christ's great might and power can flow through us until our lives become energized, moved, and aflame for God.

The important point here is that the Holy Spirit has come to make Jesus King. It seems to me that the seed, the life that was given to us when we believed—which is an eternal seed—has such resurrection power that I see a new creation rising from it with kingly qualities. Not only is the King to be within us, but also all the glories of His kingly manifestations are to be brought forth in us. Oh, for Him to work in us in this way, melting us, until a new order rises within us so that we are moved with His compassion! I see that we can come into the order of God where the vision becomes so much brighter and where the Lord is manifesting His glory with all His virtues and gifts; all His glory seems to fill the soul who is absolutely dead to himself and alive to God. There is much talk about death, but there is a death that is so deep in God that, out of that death, God brings the splendor of His life and all His glory.

An opportunity to be a flame of fire for God came when I was traveling from Egypt to Italy. What I now tell you truly happened. On the ship and everywhere, God had been with me. A man on the ship suddenly collapsed; his wife was in a terrible state, and everybody else seemed to be, too. Some said that he would die, but oh, to be a flame, to have the living Christ dwelling within you!

We are backslidden if we have to pray for power, if we have to wait until we feel a sense of His presence. The baptism of the Holy Spirit has come upon you: *"You shall receive power when the Holy Spirit has come upon you"* (Acts 1:8 NKJV). Within you is a greater power than there is in the world. (See 1 John 4:4.) Oh, to be awakened out of our unbelief into a place of daring for God on the authority of the blessed Book!

So, in the name of Jesus, I rebuked the devil, and to the astonishment of the man's wife and the man himself, he was able to stand. He said, "What is this? It is going all over me. I have never felt anything like this before." From the top of his head to the soles of his feet, the power of God shook him. God has given us authority over the power of the devil. Oh, that we may live in the place where the glory excels! It would make anyone a flame of fire.

Thought for today: When we are baptized in the Holy Spirit, it is to crown Jesus King in our lives.

DAY 51

GLORY

His divine power has given to us all things that pertain to life and godliness, through the knowledge of Him that has called us to glory and virtue.
—2 Peter 1:3

Scripture reading: 2 Peter 1:2–17

On the day of Pentecost, it was necessary that the disciples received not only the fire but also the rushing wind, the personality of the Spirit in the wind. (See Acts 2:1–4.) The manifestation of the glory is in the wind, or breath, of God.

The inward man receives the Holy Spirit instantly with great joy and blessedness. He cannot express it. Then the power of the Spirit, this breath of God, takes of the things of Jesus (see John 16:14–15) and sends forth as a river the utterances of the Spirit. Again, when the body is filled with joy, sometimes so inexpressible, the canvas of the mind has great power to move the operation of the tongue to bring out the very depths of the inward heart's power, love, and joy to us. By the same process, the Spirit, which is the breath of God, brings forth the manifestation of the glory.

Let us look at a few passages in the Bible that pertain to the glory. The first is Psalm 16:9: "*Therefore my heart is glad, and my glory rejoices.*" Something has made the rejoicing bring forth the glory. It was because the psalmist's heart was glad.

The second one is Psalm 108:1: "*O God, my heart is fixed; I will sing and give praise, even with my glory.*" You see, when the body is filled with the power of God, then the only thing that can express the glory is the tongue. Glory is presence, and the presence always comes by the tongue, which brings forth the revelations of God. God first brings His power into us.

Then He gives us verbal expressions by the same Spirit, the outward manifestation of what is within us. *"Out of the abundance of the heart the mouth speaks"* (Matthew 12:34).

Virtue has to be transmitted, and glory has to be expressed. Therefore, the Holy Spirit understands everything Christ has in the glory and brings through the heart of man God's latest thought. The world's needs, our manifestations, revivals, and all conditions are first settled in heaven, then worked out on the earth. We must be in touch with God Almighty in order to bring out on the face of the earth all the things that God has in the heavens. This is an ideal for us, and may God help us not to forsake the reality of holy communion with Him, of entering into private prayer so that publicly He may manifest His glory.

Thought for today: By filling us with the Holy Spirit, God has brought into us this glory so that out of us may come forth the glory.

DAY 52

THE MINISTRY OF THE SPIRIT

Neither count I my life dear to myself, so that I might finish my course with joy, and the ministry, which I have received of the Lord Jesus.
—Acts 20:24

Scripture reading: Romans 13:14–14:19

The ministry of the Spirit has been entrusted to us. We must be in the place of edifying the church. Law is not liberty, but if there is a move of God within you, God has written His laws in your heart so that you may delight in Him. God desires to set forth in us a perfect blending of His life and our lives so that we may have abounding inward joy—a place of reigning over all things, not a place of endeavor. There is a great difference between an endeavor and a delight.

God says to us, *"He which has called you is holy, so be you holy"* (1 Peter 1:15). Trying will never cause us to reach a place of holiness, but there is a place, or an attitude, where God gives us faith to rest on His Word, and we delight inwardly over everything. *"I delight to do Your will, O my God"* (Psalm 40:8). There is a place of great joy. Do we want condemnation?

We know there is something within that has been accomplished by the power of God, something greater than there could be in the natural order of the flesh. We are the representatives of Jesus. He was eaten up with zeal. (See John 2:17.) This intense zeal changes us by the operation of the Word; we do not rest in the letter, but we allow the blessed Holy Spirit to lift us by His power.

The disciples were with Jesus three years. He spoke out of the abundance of His heart toward them. John said, "We have touched Him; our eyes have gazed into His eyes." (See 1 John 1:1). Did Jesus know about Judas? Yes. Did He ever tell? No. When Jesus told the disciples that one of them would betray Him, they said, *"Lord, is it I?"* (Matthew 26:22). The essence of divine order is to bring the church together so that there is no schism in the body but a perfect blending of heart to heart.

"The letter kills, but the Spirit gives life" (2 Corinthians 3:6). The sword cut off Malchus's ear, but the Spirit healed it again. (See Luke 22:50–51.) Our ministry has to be in the Spirit, *"free from the law of sin and death"* (Romans 8:2). When we live in the ministry of the Spirit, we are free; in the letter, we are bound. If it is *"an eye for an eye"* (Matthew 5:38), we have lost the principle. If we are to come to a place of great liberty, the law must be at an end. Yet we love the law of God; we love to do it and not put one thing aside.

"You are manifestly declared to be the epistle of Christ ministered...with the Spirit of the living God...in fleshy tables of the heart" (2 Corinthians 3:3). It's heart worship when God has made the incision; the Spirit has come to blend with humanity.

Thought for today: Ours is not an endeavor society, but a delight to live in the will of God.

DAY 53

THE GIFTS

Now to Him that is able to keep you from falling, and to present you faultless before the presence of His glory with exceeding joy, to the only wise God our Savior, be glory and majesty, dominion and power, both now and ever. Amen.
—Jude 24–25

Scripture reading: Jude

It is very necessary that we receive the Holy Spirit in the first place; after receiving the Holy Spirit, we must earnestly desire the gifts. Then, after receiving the gifts, we must never forget that the gift is entrusted to us for bringing the blessings of God to the people.

For instance, divine healing is a gift for ministering to the needs of the people. The gift of wisdom is a word in season at the moment of need, to show you just what to do. The gift of knowledge, or the word of knowledge, is to inspire you and to bring you life and joy. This is what God intends.

Then there is the gift of discernment. We are not to discern one another but to discern evil powers and deal with them and command them back to the pit from which they came. Regarding the gift of miracles, God intends for us to come to the place where we will see miracles worked. God also wants us to understand that tongues are profitable only when they exalt and glorify the Lord. And oh, that we might really know what it means when interpretation is given! It is not merely to have beautiful sensations and think that is interpretation, but it is such that the man who has it does not know what is coming, for if he did, it would not be interpretation. Interpretation is not knowing what you are going to say, but it is being in the place where you say exactly what God says. So, when I have to interpret a message, I purposely keep my mind from anything that would hinder, and

I sometimes say "Praise the Lord" and "Hallelujah" so that everything will be a word through the Spirit, and not my word, but the word of the Lord!

We can have these divine gifts so perfectly balanced by divine love that they will be a blessing all the time. However, there is sometimes such a desire in the flesh to do something attention-getting. How the people listen and long for divine prophecy, just as interpretation comes forth! How it thrills! There is nothing wrong with it; it is beautiful. We thank God for the office and the purpose that has caused it to come, but let us be careful to finish when we are through and not continue on our own. That is how prophecy is spoiled. Don't fail, beloved, because the people know the difference. They know what is full of life, what is the real thing.

Then again, it is the same with a person praying. We love people to pray in the Holy Spirit; we love to hear them pray even the first sentences because the fire is there. However, what spoils the holiest person in prayer is when, after the spirit of prayer has gone forth, he continues on and people say, "I wish he would stop," and the church becomes silent. They say, "I wish that brother would stop. How beautifully he began; now he is dry!" But he doesn't stop.

A preacher was once having a wonderful time, and the people enjoyed it, but when he was through, he continued. A man came and said to someone at the door, "Has he finished?" "Yes," said the man, "long since, but he won't stop!" May God save us from that. People know when you are praying in the Spirit. Why should you take time and spoil everything because the natural side has come into it? God never intended that. God has a supernatural side; that is the true side, and how beautiful it is! People sometimes know better than we do, and we would also know if we were more careful.

May the Lord grant us revelation; we need discernment; we need intuition. It is the life inside. It is salvation inside, cleansing, filling; it is all inside. Revelation is inside. It is for exhibition outside, but always remember that it is inside. God's Son said as much when He said, "The pure in heart will see God." (See Matthew 5:8.) There is an inward sight of God, and it is the pure in heart who see God. Lord, keep us pure so that we will never block the way.

Thought for today: If you continue to prophesy on your own, at the end of the anointing, you are using false fire.

DAY 54

SPIRITUAL GIFTS

Now concerning spiritual gifts, brethren,
I would not have you ignorant.
—1 Corinthians 12:1

Scripture reading: Romans 11:29–12:8

God wants us to enter into the rest of faith. He desires us to have all confidence in Him. He purposes that His Word will be established in our hearts, and as we believe His Word, we will see that *"all things are possible"* (Matthew 19:26).

There is a great weakness in the church of Christ because of an awful ignorance concerning the Spirit of God and the gifts He has come to bring. God wants us to be powerful in every way because of the revelation of the knowledge of His will concerning the power and manifestation of His Spirit. He desires us to be continually hungry to receive more and more of His Spirit.

In the past, I have organized many conferences, and I have found that it is better to have a man on my platform who has not received the baptism but who is hungry for all that God has for him than a man who has received the baptism, is satisfied, has settled down, and has become stationary and stagnant. But of course, I would prefer a man who is baptized with the Holy Spirit and is still hungry for more of God.

It is impossible to overestimate the importance of being filled with the Spirit. It is impossible for us to meet the conditions of the day, to *"walk in the light, as He is in the light"* (1 John 1:7), to subdue kingdoms and work righteousness and bind the power of Satan unless we are filled with the Holy Spirit.

We read that, in the early church, *"they continued steadfastly in the apostles' doctrine and fellowship, and in breaking of bread, and in prayers"* (Acts 2:42). It is important for us also to continue steadfastly in these same things.

God wants us to understand spiritual gifts and to *"covet earnestly the best gifts"* (1 Corinthians 12:31). He also wants us to enter into the *"more excellent way"* (v. 31) of the fruit of the Spirit. We must implore God for these gifts. It is a serious thing to have the baptism and yet be stationary. We must be willing to deny ourselves everything to receive the revelation of God's truth and to receive the fullness of the Spirit. Only that will satisfy God, and nothing less must satisfy us.

I knew a man who was full of the Holy Spirit and would only preach when he knew that he was mightily anointed by the power of God. He was once asked to preach at a Methodist church. He was staying at the minister's house, and he said, "You go on to church, and I will follow." The place was packed with people, but this man did not show up. The Methodist minister, becoming anxious, sent his little girl to inquire why he did not come. As she came to the bedroom door, she heard him crying out three times, "I will not go." She went back and reported that she had heard the man say three times that he would not go. The minister was troubled about it, but almost immediately afterward, the man came in. As he preached that night, the power of God was tremendously manifested. The preacher later asked him, "Why did you tell my daughter that you were not coming?" He answered, "I know when I am filled. I am an ordinary man, and I told the Lord that I did not dare to go and would not go until He gave me a fresh filling of the Spirit. The moment the glory filled me and overflowed, I came to the meeting."

Yes, there is a power, a blessing, an assurance, a rest in the presence of the Holy Spirit. You can feel His presence and know that He is with you. You do not need to spend an hour without this inner knowledge of His holy presence. With His power upon you, there can be no failure. You are above par all the time.

Thought for today: Many people today are in the midst of a great river of life but are dying of thirst because they do not dip down and take it.

DAY 55

PENTECOSTAL POWER

Grow in grace, and in the knowledge of our Lord and Savior Jesus Christ.
—2 Peter 3:18

Scripture reading: Hebrews 12:12–24

When I think about Pentecost, I am astonished from day to day because of its mightiness, its wonderfulness, and how the glory overshadows it. I think sometimes about these things, and they make me feel that we have only just touched the surface of it. Truly it is so, but we must thank God that we have touched it. We must not give in because we have only touched the surface. Whatever God has done in the past, His name is still the same. When hearts are burdened and they come face-to-face with the need of the day, they look into God's Word, and it brings in a propeller of power or an anointing that makes them know that He has truly visited.

It was a wonderful day when Jesus left the glory to come to earth. I can imagine God the Father and all the angels and all heaven so wonderfully stirred that day when the angels were sent to tell the wonderful story of "peace on earth and goodwill to men." (See Luke 2:14.) It was a glorious day when they beheld Jesus for the first time and God was looking on. I suppose it would take a big book to contain all that happened after that day up until Jesus was thirty years old. Everything in His life was working up to a great climax. The mother of Jesus hid many of these things in her heart. (See v. 19.)

I know that Pentecost in my life is working up to a climax; it is not all accomplished in a day. There are many waters and all kinds of experiences that we go through before we get to the real summit of everything. The power of God is here to prevail. God is with us.

Thought for today: When the Spirit of God is waiting at your heart's door, do not resist Him; instead, open your heart to the touch of God.

DAY 56

SPIRITUAL WARFARE

For the weapons of our warfare are not carnal, but mighty through God to the pulling down of strong holds.
—2 Corinthians 10:4

Scripture reading: 2 Corinthians 10:1–6

People ask, "Do all speak with tongues?" Certainly not. But all people may speak as the Spirit gives utterance—as in the Upper Room and at the house of Cornelius and at Ephesus when Jesus's followers were filled with the Holy Spirit.

There is quite a difference between having a gift and speaking as the Spirit gives utterance. If I had been given the gift of tongues when I was filled with the Holy Spirit, then I could have spoken in tongues at any time, because gifts and calling remain. (See Romans 11:29.) But I couldn't speak in tongues after I was baptized. Why? It was because I had received the Holy Spirit with the evidence of speaking in tongues, but I hadn't received the gift of tongues.

However, I received the Holy Spirit, who is the Giver of all gifts, and nine months afterward, God gave me the gift of tongues so that I could speak in tongues at any time. But do I? God forbid! Why? Because no man ought to use a gift; the Holy Spirit uses the gift.

I have a reason for talking like this. People come up to me all the time and say, "I have been prayed for, and I am just the same." It is enough to make you kick them. I don't mean that literally. I would be the last man to kick anybody in this place. God forbid. But if I can get you enraged against the powers of darkness and the powers of disease, if I can wake you up, you won't go to bed unless you prove that there is a Master in you who is greater than the power that is hanging around you.

Many times I have gone to a house in which an insane person lived and have been shut in with him in order to deliver him. I have gone in determined that he would be delivered. In the middle of the night chiefly, or sometimes in the middle of the day, the demon powers would come and bite me and handle me terribly roughly. But I never gave in. It would dethrone a higher principle if I had to give in.

May the God of grace and mercy strengthen us. In the measure that we destroy these evil powers, we make it easier for weak believers. For every time Satan overcomes a saint, it gives him ferocity for another attack; but when he is subdued, he will come to the place where defeat is written against him.

In your home, with your spouse and children, you will have audacity of determination, along with a righteous indignation, against the power of disease, to cast it out. That is worth more to you than anything you could buy.

Thought for today: No one can have a knowledge of an inward Christ without having a longing that there will be an increase of souls saved.

DAY 57

USE THE GIFTS WISELY

We labor, that...we may be accepted of him.
—2 Corinthians 5:9

Scripture reading: 2 Corinthians 5:1–17

While it is right to earnestly desire the best gifts, you must recognize that the all-important thing is to be filled with the power of the Holy Spirit Himself. You will never have trouble with people who are filled with the power of the Holy Spirit, but you will have a lot of trouble with people who have the gifts but no power. The Lord does not want us to *"come short"* in any gift (1 Corinthians 1:7 NKJV), but at the same time, He wants us to be so filled with the Holy Spirit that it will be the Holy Spirit manifesting Himself through the gifts. Where the glory of God alone is desired, you can expect that every gift that is needed will be made manifest. To glorify God is better than to idolize gifts. We prefer the Spirit of God to any gift, but we can see the manifestation of the Trinity in the gifts: different gifts but the same Spirit, different administrations but the same Lord, diversities of operation but the same God working all in all. (See 1 Corinthians 12:4–6.) Can you conceive of what it will mean for our triune God to be manifesting Himself in His fullness in our assemblies?

Imagine a large locomotive boiler that is being filled with steam. You can see the engine letting off some of the steam as it remains stationary. It looks as though the whole thing might burst. You can see believers who are like that. They start to scream, but that does not edify anyone. However, when the locomotive moves on, it serves the purpose for which it was built and pulls along many cars with goods in them. It is the same way with believers when they are operating in the gifts of the Spirit properly.

When you have a good time, you must see that the spiritual conditions in the place lend themselves to it and that the people are falling in line with you. Then you will always find it a blessing.

Thought for today: We must be careful not to have a good time in the Lord at the expense of somebody else.

DAY 58

WHAT IS YOUR MOTIVE?

You ask, and receive not, because you ask amiss,
that you may consume it upon your lusts.
—James 4:3

Scripture reading: Ephesians 1:3–14

God says, "*Everyone who asks receives*" (Matthew 7:8 NKJV). What are you asking for? What is your motive? There is a need for the gifts, and God will reveal to you what you ought to have, and you should never be satisfied until you receive it.

It is important that we know we can do nothing in ourselves. However, we may know that we are clothed with the power of God so that, in a sense, we are not in the natural man. As we go forth in this power, things will take place as they took place in the days of the disciples.

When I received the new birth at eight years of age, it was so precious and lovely. Since that time, I have never lost the knowledge of my acceptance with God. Then, brothers and sisters, God did a wonderful work in me when I waited for the baptism.

I was in a strange position. For sixteen years I had testified to having received the baptism of the Holy Spirit, but I had really only received the anointing of the Spirit. In fact, I could not preach unless I had the anointing. My wife would come to me and say, "They are waiting for you to come out and speak to the people." I would say, "I cannot and will not come without the anointing of the Spirit."

I can see now that I was calling the anointing the baptism. But when the Holy Spirit came into my body, until I could not give satisfaction to the glory that was in me, God took this tongue, and I spoke as the Spirit gave utterance, which brought perfect satisfaction to me. When He comes in, He abides. I then began to reach out as the Holy Spirit showed me.

Thought for today: We must be willing to deny ourselves everything to receive the revelation of God's truth and to receive the fullness of the Spirit. Only this will satisfy God, and nothing less must satisfy us.

DAY 59

CLAIM THE GIFT

I pray you, let a double portion of your spirit be upon me.
—2 Kings 2:9

Scripture reading: 2 Kings 2:1–14

In the call of the prophet Elisha, God saw the young man's willingness to obey. The twelve yoke of oxen, the plow, and all soon came to nothing; all bridges had to be burned behind him. (See 1 Kings 19:19–21.) Friend, the Lord has called you, too. Are you separated from the old things? You cannot go on unless you are.

As Elisha went on with the prophet Elijah, the young man heard wonderful things about Elijah's ministry, and he longed for the time when he would take his master's place. Now the time was getting close. His master said to him, "I am going to Gilgal today. I want you to remain here." "Master," he replied, "I must go with you." Other people also knew something about it, for they said to Elisha, "Do you know that your master is going to be taken away from you today?" He said, "Hold your peace; I know it." Later on, Elijah said, "I want to go on to Bethel. You stay here." But Elisha said, "No, I will not leave you." Something had been revealed to Elisha. Perhaps, in a similar way, God is drawing you to do something; you feel it.

Then Elijah said, "The Lord has sent me to Jordan. You stay here." It was the spirit of the old man that was stirring up the young man. If you see zeal in somebody else, reach out for it; it is for you. I am coming to realize that God wants all the members of His body joined together. In these days He is making us feel that when a person is failing to go on with God, we must restore that member.

When they came to the Jordan, Elijah struck his cloak on it and they crossed. No doubt Elisha said, "I must follow his steps." And when they had gone over, the old man said, "You have done well; you would not stay back. What is the real desire of your heart? I feel I am going to leave you. Ask what you like now, before I leave you." "Master," he said, "I have seen all that you have done. Master, I want twice as much as you have."

I believe it is the fainthearted who do not get much. As they went on up the hill, down came the chariot of fire, nearer and nearer, and when it landed, the old man jumped in and the young man said, "Father, Father, Father," and down came the cloak.

What have you asked for? Are you satisfied to continue on in the old way now that the Holy Spirit has come to give you an unlimited supply of power and says, "What will you have?" Why, we see that Peter was so filled with the Holy Spirit that his shadow falling on sick people healed them. (See Acts 5:15.)

What do you want? Elisha asked, and he got it. He came down and said, "I don't feel any differently." However, he had the knowledge that feelings are not to be counted as anything; some of you are looking at your feelings all the time. He came to the waters of the Jordan as an ordinary man. Then, in the knowledge in which he possessed the cloak (not in any feelings about it), he said, "Where is the God of Elijah?" and he struck the water with the cloak. The waters parted, and Elisha put his feet down in the river and crossed to the other side. When you put your feet down and say you are going to have a double portion, you will get it. After he had crossed, there were the young men again (they always come where there is power), and they said, "*The spirit of Elijah rests on Elisha*" (2 Kings 2:15 NKJV).

You are to have the gifts and to claim them. The Lord will certainly change your lives, and you will be new men and women. Are you asking for a double portion? I trust that no one will "*come short*" in any gift (1 Corinthians 1:7 NKJV). You say, "I have asked. Do you think God will be pleased if I ask again?" Yes, do so before Him. Ask again, and we may go forth in the Spirit of the cloak. Then we will no longer be working in our own strength but in the Holy Spirit's strength, and we will see and know His power because we believe.

Thought for today: Many people miss a great many things because they are always thinking that they are for someone else.

DAY 60

THE WORD OF WISDOM

To one is given by the Spirit the word of wisdom.
—1 Corinthians 12:8

Scripture reading: 1 Corinthians 2:6–16

The Scripture does not say "the gift of wisdom" but the gift of *"the word of wisdom."* You have to *"rightly* [handle] *the word of truth"* (2 Timothy 2:15). The gift of the word of wisdom is necessary in many instances. For example, when you want to build another church building, maybe larger than the one you are in, so that everybody can speak and be heard without any trouble, a word of wisdom is needed regarding how to build the place for God's service.

When you are faced with a choice and it is difficult for you to know in what direction to go, that word can come to you in a moment and prepare you for the right way.

The gift of the word of wisdom is meant for a needy hour when you are under great stress concerning some business transaction; provided it is a godly transaction, you can ask God what to do, and you will receive wisdom.

I have been trying to show you that if you are filled with the Holy Spirit, the Holy Spirit can manifest any gift. At the same time, you are not to forget that the Word of God urges you to desire earnestly the best gifts; so, while the best gift might be to you the word of wisdom, or some other gift, you should not be lacking in any gift.

This is a remarkable statement for me to make, but Scripture lends itself to me to be extravagant. When God speaks to me, He says, "Anything you ask." (See John 15:7.) When God is speaking of the world's salvation,

He says, *"whosoever believes"* (John 3:16). So, I have an extravagant God with extravagant language to make me an extravagant person—in wisdom.

To this end, we pray that God will show us now why we really need the word of wisdom and how we may be in a place in which we will surely know it is of God.

Thought for today: The trouble with so many people is that they have never gotten out so He could get in.

DAY 61

THE GIFTS OF HEALING

To another the gifts of healing by the same Spirit.
—1 Corinthians 12:9

Scripture reading: Psalm 65

Now I will deal with the gift itself. It is actually "gifts" of healing, not the "gift" of healing. Gifts of healing can deal with every case of sickness, every disease that there is. These gifts are so full that they are beyond human expression, but you come into the fullness of them as the light brings revelation to you.

I have people continually coming to me and saying, "When you are preaching, I see a halo around you," or "When you are preaching, I have seen angels standing around you."

I hear these things from time to time, and I am thankful that people have such spiritual vision. I do not have that kind of vision; however, I have the express glory, the glory of the Lord, covering me, the intense inner working of His power, until every time I have stood before people, I have known that I have not had to choose the words I have spoken. The language has been chosen, the thoughts have been chosen, and I have been speaking in prophecy more than in any other way, so that I know we have been in the school of the Holy Spirit in a great way.

The only vision I have had in a divine healing meeting is this: so often, when I have laid hands upon the people, I have seen two hands go before my hands. This has happened many, many times.

The person who has the gifts of healing does not look to see what is happening. You will notice that after I have finished ministering, many things are manifested, but they don't move me. I am not moved by anything I see.

The divine gifts of healing are so profound in the person who has them that there is no such thing as doubt, and there could not be; whatever happens could not change the person's opinion or thought or act. He expects the very thing that God intends him to have as he lays hands upon the seeker.

Wherever I go, the manifestation of divine healing is considerably greater after I leave than when I am there. Why? It is God's plan for me. God has great grace over me. Wonderful things have been accomplished, and people have told me what happened when I was there, but these things were hidden from me. God has a reason why He hides things from me.

When I lay hands upon people for a specific thing, I tell you, that thing will take place. I believe it will be so, and I never turn my ears or my eyes from the fact. It has to be so.

The gifts of divine healing are more than audacity; they are more than an unction. Those are two big things; however, the gifts of healing are the solid fact of a divine nature within the person pressing forward—the very nature and activity of the Lord, as if He were there. We are in this place to glorify the Father, and the Father will be glorified in the Son since we are not afraid of taking action in this day.

The gifts of healing are a fact. They are a production; they are a faith; they are an unwavering trust; they are a confidence; they are a reliability.

People sometimes come to me very troubled. They say, "I had the gifts of healing once, but something has happened, and I do not have them now."

They never had them. "*The gifts and the calling of God are irrevocable*" (Romans 11:29 NKJV), and they remain under every circumstance except this: if you fall from grace and use a gift, it will work against you. If you use tongues out of the will of God, interpretation will condemn you. If you have been used and the gift has been exercised, and then you have fallen from your high place, it will work against you.

Thought for today: If you are without condemnation, you are in a place where you can pray through.

DAY 62

TESTIMONIAL PROPHECY

And I fell at his feet to worship him. And he said to me,
See you do it not: I am your fellow-servant, and of your brethren that
have the testimony of Jesus: worship God:
for the testimony of Jesus is the spirit of prophecy.
—Revelation 19:10

Scripture reading: Revelation 19

There is the prophecy that is the testimony of the saved person regarding what Jesus has done for him. Everyone, every newborn soul, has this kind of prophecy. Through the new birth that results in righteousness, God has given an anointing of the Spirit, a real unction of the Spirit of Christ. We felt when we were saved that we wanted everybody to be saved. That mindset has to be continuous; the whole world can be regenerated by the spirit of prophecy as we testify of our salvation in Christ.

This is the same prophecy that Paul spoke about in 1 Corinthians 14:1: *"Follow after charity, and desire spiritual gifts, but rather that you may prophesy."* This verse identifies prophecy as being more important than other gifts. Think about that: prophecy is to be chosen and desired above all the other gifts; the greatest among all the gifts is prophecy.

Why prophecy? Because prophecy by the power of the Spirit is the only power that saves humanity. We are told in the Word of God that the gospel that is presented through prophecy has power to bring immortality and light. (See 2 Timothy 1:10.) Immortality is what abides forever. Light is what opens the understanding of your heart. Light and immortality come by the gospel.

Prophecy is to be desired above all things, and every Christian has to have it. Every believer may have gifts, though there are very few who do; however, every believer has testimonial prophecy.

Looking at Revelation 19:10, let us see what testimonial prophecy is and how it comes forth. *"I fell at his feet."* Who is this inhabitant of heaven? The one speaking to John is a man who has been on the earth. Lots of people are foolishly led by the devil to believe that, after they die, their spirits will be asleep in the grave; this is absolutely contrary to the Word of God. Don't you know that even if you live until the Lord comes, the body that you have must be put off and another must be put on, because you cannot go into heaven with your present body? (See 1 Corinthians 15:33.)

This man has been in the earth in the body and is now in heaven in the spirit, and he wants you to hear what he has to say: *"I am your fellow-servant, and of your brethren that have the testimony of Jesus...for the testimony of Jesus is the spirit of prophecy."* What is the testimony of Jesus? The testimony is: "Jesus has saved me." What the world wants to know today is how they can be saved.

Testify that you are saved. Your knees may knock together, you may be trembling as you do it, but when you get it out, you enter into the spirit of prophecy. Before you know where you are, you are saying things that the Spirit is saying.

There are thousands of Christians who have never received the baptism of the Holy Spirit but who have this wonderful spirit of prophecy. People are being saved everywhere by the testimony of such believers. If you cease from testifying, you will be sorry when you give an account of your life before God. (See Romans 14:12.) As you testify, you will be a vessel through which the power of God can bring salvation to people. (See Romans 1:16.) Testify wherever you are.

Live in the place where the Lord your God moves you, not to go from house to house nor speak from person to person, but where the Lord directs you, for He has the person who is in need of truth waiting for watering with your watering can. Do not forget that you are *"ambassadors for Christ"* (2 Corinthians 5:20).

Thought for today: The spirit of prophecy is the testimony that you are saved by the blood of the Lamb.

DAY 63

DISCERNMENT VERSUS JUDGING

To another discerning of spirits.
—1 Corinthians 12:10

Scripture reading: Romans 2:1–16

Discernment is a very necessary gift to understand. Most people seem to think it is a discerning of human persons. It is amazing to find that many people I come across seem to have a tremendous bent toward "discerning" others. If you carefully put this discerning of one another into real practice upon yourself for twelve months, you will never presume to try it upon another. You will see so many faults about yourself that you will say, "O God, make me right!"

There is a vast difference between natural discernment and spiritual discernment. This statement of Jesus is remarkable:

> *How will you say to your brother, Let me pull out the mote out of your eye; and, behold, a beam is in your own eye? You hypocrite, first cast out the beam out of your own eye; and then shall you see clearly to cast out the mote out of your brother's eye.* (Matthew 7:4–5)

Remember that if you begin judging, it will lead you to judgment (vv. 1–2). If you begin using your discernment to weigh people by your standards, it will lead you to judgment. Ever since God showed me Romans 2:1–3, I have been very careful to examine myself before I begin judging. Balance that in your heart. It will save you from judging.

Many notable people in the world have gotten to running another person down and finding fault. They are always prone to faultfinding and judging people outright. I find that those people always fall in the mire. If I were to mention these people by name, you would know that what I am saying is true.

God save us from criticism! When we are pure in heart, we only think about pure things. When we are impure in heart, we speak and act and think as we are in our hearts. The pure in heart see purity.

Thought for today: May God give us that inward desire for purity so that He can take away judging.

DAY 64

DISCERNING SPIRITS

Beloved, believe not every spirit,
but try the spirits whether they are of God.
—1 John 4:1

Scripture reading: 1 John 4:1–11

From time to time, as I have seen a person under a power of evil or having a fit, I have said to the satanic force that is within the possessed person, "Did Jesus Christ come in the flesh?" and right away they have answered no. They either say no or hold their tongues, refusing altogether to acknowledge that the Lord Jesus Christ came in the flesh. It is at a time like this when, remembering that further statement of John's, "*Greater is He that is in you, than he that is in the world*" (1 John 4:4), you can, in the name of the Lord Jesus Christ, deal with the evil powers and command them to come out. We must know the tactics of the Evil One, and we must be able to displace and dislodge him from his position.

In Australia, I went to one place where there were disrupted and broken homes. The people were so deluded by the evil power of Satan that men had left their wives and wives had left their husbands. That is the devil! May God deliver us from such evils in these days. There is no one better than the companion God has given you. I have seen so many broken hearts and so many homes that have been wrecked. We need a real revelation of these evil seducing spirits who come in and fascinate through the eyes, and who destroy lives, bringing the work of God into disrepute. There is always flesh behind it. It is never clean. It is unholy, impure, satanic, devilish—and hell is behind it. If the Enemy comes in to tempt you in any way like this, I implore you to look instantly to the Lord Jesus. He can deliver you from any such satanic power. You must be separated in every way if you are going to have faith.

The Holy Spirit will give us this gift of the discerning of spirits if we desire it. Then we will be able to perceive by revelation evil powers that come in to destroy. We can reach out and get this unction of the Spirit that will reveal these things to us.

Seek the Lord, and He will sanctify every thought, every action, until your whole being is ablaze with holy purity and your one desire is for Him who has created you in holiness. Oh, this holiness! Can we be made pure? We can. Every inbred sin must go. God can cleanse away every evil thought. Can we have a hatred for sin and a love for righteousness? Yes, God will create within you a pure heart. He will take away your stony heart and give you a heart of flesh. He will sprinkle you with clean water, and you will be cleansed from all your filthiness. (See Ezekiel 36:25–26.) When will He do it? When you seek Him for such inward purity.

Thought for today: To discern spirits, we must dwell with Him who is holy, and He will give the revelation and unveil the mask of satanic power, whatever it is.

DAY 65

DELIVERANCE

Come out of the man, you unclean spirit.
—Mark 5:8

Scripture reading: Mark 5:1–20

Let me tell you what may seem to be a horrible story for you to hear; nevertheless, it is a situation in which discernment is necessary. This is happening all the time, and I do thank God for it because it is teaching me how to minister to people in the Lord.

Messages came to me again and again by telegraph, letters, and other things, asking that I come to London. I wired back and wrote, but so many calls came, and no hint was given in any way as to the reason I was to go there. The only thing they said was that they were in great distress.

When I got there, the dear father and mother of the needy one both took me by the hand and broke down and wept.

"Surely this is deep sorrow of heart," I said.

They led me up onto the balcony. Then they pointed to a door that was open a little, and both of them left me. I went in that door, and I have never seen a sight like it in all my life. I saw a young woman who was beautiful to look at, but she had four big men holding her down to the floor, and her clothing was torn from the struggle.

When I got into the room and looked into her eyes, her eyes rolled but she could not speak. She was exactly like the man in the Bible who came out of the tombs and ran to Jesus when he saw Him. As soon as he got to Jesus, he couldn't speak, but the demon powers spoke. (See Mark 5:1–13.) And the demon powers in this young girl spoke and said, "I know you. You can't cast us out; we are many."

"Yes," I said, "I know you are many, but my Lord Jesus will cast you all out."

It was a wonderful moment; it was a moment when it was He alone who could do it.

The power of Satan was so great upon this beautiful girl that she whirled and broke away from these four strong men.

The Spirit of the Lord was wonderful in me, and I went right up to her and looked into her face. I saw the evil powers there; her very eyes flashed with demon power.

"In the name of Jesus," I said, "I command you to leave. Though you are many, I command you to leave this moment, in the name of Jesus."

She instantly became sick and began vomiting. She vomited out thirty-seven evil spirits and gave their names as they came out. That day she was made as perfect as anybody. Praise the Lord!

Thought for today: The gift of discernment is not criticism.

DAY 66

THE HOLY SPIRIT VERSUS DECEPTIVE VOICES

Hereby know you the Spirit of God: Every spirit that confesses that Jesus Christ is come in the flesh is of God: And every spirit that confesses not that Jesus Christ is come in the flesh is not of God.
—1 John 4:2–3

Scripture reading: 1 John 4:1–6

A lot of people are troubled by voices. Some are so troubled that they become very distressed. Some people take it as a great thing; they think it is very remarkable, and they go astray. Lots of people go astray by foolish prophecy, and many are foolish enough to believe that they have tongues and interpretation and that they can be told what they should do. This is altogether outside the plan of God and bordering on blasphemy.

I do not preach my own ideas. That is, I never tell you what I think, because everybody can think. I tell you what I know. Therefore, what you need to do is to listen to what I know so that you may learn it. Then you can tell others what you have learned so that they will learn also.

How can I dislodge the power of Satan? How can I deal with satanic power? How may I know whether a voice is of God or not? Are there not voices that come from God? Yes. I am here believing that I am in the right place to build you on the authority of the Word of God.

You know that a business executive is one who has a right to declare everything for the board of directors. And the Chief Executive of the world is the Holy Spirit. He is here today as a communication to our hearts, to our minds, to our thoughts, of what God wants us to know. So, this Holy Executive who is in us can speak wonderful words.

I am dealing now with what you may know when you are fully in the Holy Spirit. The Spirit will teach you; He will *"bring all things to your remembrance"* (John 14:26). Now you do not need any man to teach you, but the anointing remains. (See 1 John 2:27.) This is the office of the Holy Spirit. This is the power of His communication. This is what John meant when he said, *"God is love"* (1 John 4:8). Jesus, who is grace, is with you—but the Holy Spirit is the speaker, and He speaks everything concerning Jesus.

There may be people who have been hearing voices, and it has put them in situations that have caused tremendous issues in their lives, brought a great amount of distress and heartbreak, and led them into confusion and trouble. Why? They did not know how to judge the voices.

If a voice comes and tells you what to do, if a person comes and says he has a special prophecy that God has given him for you, you have as much right to ask God for that prophecy as they had to give it to you, and you have as much right to judge that prophecy according to the Word of God. You need to do this, for there are people going about pretending to be tremendous people, and they are sending people to be nearly at their wits' end because they believe their damnable prophecies, which never are of God but are of the devil. I am very severe on this thing. God won't let me rest; I have to deal with these things because I find people everywhere in a terrible state because of these voices. How will we get to know the difference between the voice of God and the voice of Satan? The Scripture tells us. (See 1 John 4:2–3.)

Thought for today: You do not need teachers, but you need the Teacher, who is the Holy Spirit, to bring all things to your remembrance.

DAY 67

WHY TONGUES?

Wherefore tongues are for a sign, not to them that believe, but to them that believe not:
—1 Corinthians 14:22

Scripture reading: 1 Corinthians 14:26–40

Why has God brought this gift of tongues into operation? There is a reason. If there were not a reason, it would not be there. Why did God design it? You must see with me that the gift of tongues was never in evidence before the Holy Spirit came. The old dispensation was very wonderful in prophetic utterances. Every person, whoever he is, who receives the Holy Spirit will have prophetic utterances in the Spirit unto God or in a human language supernaturally coming forth, so that all the people will know that it is the Spirit.

This is the reason we want all the people filled with the Holy Spirit: they are to be prophetic. When a prophecy is given, it means that God has a thought, a word in season, that has never been in season before—things both new and old. The Holy Spirit brings things to pass!

So, when God fulfilled the promise, when the time was appointed, the Holy Spirit came and filled the apostles. The gift that had never been in operation before came into operation that wonderful day in the Upper Room, and for the first time in all of history, men were speaking in a new order; it was not an old language, but language that was to be interpreted.

This is profound because we recognize that God is speaking. No man understands it. The Spirit is speaking, and the Spirit opens the revelation that they will have, without adulteration.

Tongues are a wonderful display of this; they are to revive the people; they are to give new depths of thought.

If you ever want to know why the Holy Spirit was greatly needed, you will find it in the third chapter of Ephesians. You will be amazed. The language is wonderful. Paul said that he was *"the least of all saints"* (Ephesians 3:8), yet God had called him to be a *"minister"* (v. 7). His language is wonderful, yet he felt in his heart and life that there was something greater, that the Spirit had him, and he bowed his *"knees to the Father"* (v. 14).

You cannot find in all the Scriptures words with such profound fruit as those that ring through the verses of Paul's remarkable prayer in the Holy Spirit. He prayed *"that you might be filled with all the fullness of God"* (v. 19) and *"that you...may be able to comprehend with all saints"* (vv. 17–18). He prayed that you may be able to ask and think, and think and ask, and that it will not only be abundantly but that it will also be *"exceeding abundantly above all that"* you can *"ask or think"* (v. 20). There is a man closing down and the Holy Spirit praying.

Thought for today: The Holy Spirit did not come to exalt you; He came so that you could exalt the Lord.

DAY 68

HUMILITY AND COMPASSION

And being found in fashion as a man, He humbled Himself, and became obedient to death, even the death of the cross.
—Philippians 2:8

Scripture reading: Philippians 2:1–18

It is very important to minister in the gifts of the Spirit in the proper way. There is no anointing like the unction that comes out of death, when we are dead with Christ. It is this position that makes us live with Him. If we have been conformed to His death, then, in that same death, like Paul, we will be made like Him in His resurrection power. (See Philippians 3:10–11.)

But do not forget that Jesus was coequal with the Father and that He made Himself of no reputation when he became man and came to earth. (See Philippians 2:6–7.) He did not come out and say that He was this, that, or the other. No, that was not His position. Jesus had all the gifts. He could have stood up and said to Peter and John and James and the rest of them, when the dead son was being carried through the gate of the city of Nain (see Luke 7:11–15), "Stand to one side, Peter. Clear out of the way, John. Make room for Me, Thomas. Don't you know who I am? I am coequal with the Father. I have all power, I have all gifts, I have all graces. Stand to one side; I will show you how to raise the dead!"

Is that how He did it? No! Never. Then what made it come to pass? He was observant. The disciples were there, but they did not have the same observance. What did He see? He saw the widow and knew that she was carrying to burial that day all her help, all her life. Her love was bound up in that son. There she was, broken and bent over with sorrow, all her hopes blighted.

Jesus had compassion upon her, and the compassion of Jesus was greater than death. His compassion was so marvelous that it went beyond the powers of death and all the powers of demons. Isn't He a lovely Jesus? Isn't He a precious Savior?

Thought for today: Observance comes from an inward holy flame kindled by God.

DAY 69

A PERFECT WAY

Though I speak with the tongues of men and of angels, and have not charity, I am become as sounding brass, or a tinkling cymbal.
—1 Corinthians 13:1

Scripture reading: 1 Corinthians 13

Did you ever read a verse like this? It is the state of being brought into a treasury. Do you know what a treasury is? A treasury holds or handles priceless things.

God puts you into the treasury to hold or handle the precious gifts of the Spirit. Therefore, so that you may not fail to handle them correctly, He gives you a picture of how you may handle them.

What a high position of authority, of grace, the Lord speaks about in this verse! "*Speak with the tongues of men and of angels.*" Oh, isn't that wonderful!

There are men who have such wonderful qualifications for speaking. Their knowledge in the natural realm is so outstanding that many people go to hear their eloquent addresses because the language in them is so beautiful. Yet, through the baptism in the Holy Spirit, God puts you right in the midst of them and says that He has given you the capability to speak like men, with power of thought and language at your disposal, so that you can say anything.

People are failing God all the time all over the world because they are taken up with their own eloquence, and God is not in it. They are lost with the pretentiousness of their great authority over language, and they use it on purpose to tickle the ears and the sensations of the people, and it profits nothing. It is nothing. It will wither up, and the people who use it will wither up.

Yet God has said there is a way. Now, how would language *"of men and of angels"* come to prosper?

When you wept through to victory before, you were able to do anything. You were so undone that unless God helped you to do it, you couldn't do it. You were so broken in spirit that your whole body seemed to be at an end unless God reinstated you. Then the unction came, and every word was glorifying Jesus. Every sentence lifted the people, and they felt as they listened, "Surely God is in this place! He has sent His Word and healed us." (See Psalm 107:20.) They saw no man there except Jesus. Jesus was so manifested that they all said, "Oh, wasn't Jesus speaking to our hearts this morning!"

If you minister in this way, you will never become nothing. Tongues of men and angels alone will come to nothing. Yet if you speak with tongues of men and angels that are bathed in the love of God until it is to Him alone that you speak, then it will be written down forever in the history of the glory. So, let the Lord help us to know how to act in the Holy Spirit.

Thought for today: When you are used only for and desire only the glory of God, your acts, life, ministry, and power will be recorded endlessly in the glory of heaven—for the acts of the apostles are being recorded in the glory.

DAY 70

ABIDE IN CHRIST

I am the vine, you are the branches: He that abides in Me,
and I in him, the same brings forth much fruit:
for without Me you can do nothing.
—John 15:5

Scripture reading: John 15:1–17

Beloved, it is lovely to be in the will of God. Now then, how may we be something? By just being nothing, by receiving the Holy Spirit, by being in the place where we can be directed by God and filled with His power.

What it must be to have speaking ability, to have a beautiful language, as so many men have! It is wonderful to have the tongue of an angel so that all the people who hear you are moved by your use of language. Yet how I would weep, how my heart would be broken, if I came to speak before you in beautiful language without the power.

If I had an angel's language and the people were all taken with what I said, but Jesus was not glorified at all, it would all be hopeless, barren, and unfruitful. I myself should be nothing. But if I speak and say, "Lord, let them hear Your voice. Lord, let them be compelled to hear Your truth. Lord, anyhow, any way, hide me today"—then He becomes glorious, and all the people say, "We have seen Jesus!"

When I was in California, I spent many days with our dear Brother Montgomery when I had a chance. During this time, a man wrote to Brother Montgomery. This man had been saved but had lost his joy; he had lost all he had. He wrote, "I am through with everything. I am not going to touch this thing again; I am through." Brother Montgomery wrote back to him and said, "I will never try to persuade you again if you will hear once. There is a man from England, and if you will only hear him once, I will pay all your expenses." So, he came. He listened, and at the end of the time, he said to me, "This is the truth I am telling you. I have seen the Lord standing beside you, and I heard His voice. I never even saw you.

"I have a lot of money," he continued, "and I have a valley five hundred miles long. If you speak the word to me, I will go on your word, and I will open that valley for the Lord."

I have preached in several of his places, and God has used him wonderfully to speak throughout that valley. What I would have missed when he came the first day if I had been trying to say something of my own instead of the Lord being there and speaking His words through me! Never let us do anything to lose this divine love, this close affection in our hearts that says, "Not I, but Christ; not I, but Christ!"

Lose all your identity in the Son of God. Let Him become all in all. Seek only the Lord, and let Him be glorified. You will have gifts; you will have grace and wisdom. God is waiting for the person who will lay all on the altar, fiftytwo weeks in the year, three hundred and sixtyfive days in the year, and then continue perpetually in the Holy Spirit.

Thought for today: Forget yourself and get lost in Him.

DAY 71

A PERFECT FIT

There are diversities of gifts, but the same Spirit.
—1 Corinthians 12:4

Scripture reading: Romans 12:3–13

The variation among humanity is tremendous. Faces are different, so are physiques. Your whole body may be put together in such a way that one particular gift would not suit you at all, while it would suit another person.

So, the Word of God deals here with varieties of gifts, meaning that these gifts perfectly meet the condition of each believer. That is God's plan. It may be that not one person would be led to claim all the gifts. Nevertheless, do not be afraid; the Scriptures are definite. Paul said that you do not need to come short in any gift. (See 1 Corinthians 1:7.) God has wonderful things for you beyond what you have ever known. The Holy Spirit is so full of prophetic operations of divine power that it is marvelous what may happen after the Holy Spirit comes.

How He loosed me! I am no good without the Holy Spirit. The power of the Holy Spirit loosed my language. I was like my mother. She had no ability to speak. If she began to tell a story, she couldn't finish it. My father would say, "Mother, you will have to begin again." I was like that. I couldn't tell a story. I was bound. I had plenty of thoughts, but no language. But oh, after the Holy Spirit came!

When He came, I had a great desire for gifts. The Lord caused me to see that it is possible for every believer to live in such holy anointing, such divine communion, such presseddown measure (see Luke 6:38) by the power of the Spirit, that every gift can be his.

But is there not a vast and appalling unconcern about possessing the gifts? You may ask a score of believers, chosen at random from almost any church, "Do you have any of the gifts of the Spirit?" The answer from all will be, "No," and it will be given in a tone and with a manner that conveys the thought that the believer is not surprised that he does not have the gifts, that he doesn't expect to have any of them, and that he does not expect to seek them. Isn't this terrible, when the living Word specifically exhorts us to *"earnestly desire the best gifts"* (1 Corinthians 12:31 NKJV)?

In order that the gifts might be everything and in evidence, we have to see that we cease to live without His glory. He works with us, and we work with Him—cooperating, working together. This is divine. Surely this is God's plan.

God has brought you to the banquet, and He wants to send you away full. We are in a place where God wants to give us visions. We are in a place where, in His great love, He is bending over us with kisses. Oh, how lovely is the kiss of Jesus, the expression of His love!

Oh, come, let us seek Him for the best gifts, and let us strive to be wise and to rightly divide the Word of Truth (see 2 Timothy 2:15), giving it forth in power so that the church may be edified and sinners may be saved.

Thought for today: Look to the Holy Spirit to show you how to use the gifts so that you never use them without the power of the Spirit.

DAY 72

YIELD TO THE HOLY SPIRIT

Wherefore, brethren, covet to prophesy, and forbid not to speak with tongues. Let all things be done decently and in order.
—1 Corinthians 14:39–40

Scripture reading: 1 Corinthians 14:1–25

You are not to consider, under any circumstances, that, because you have a spiritual gift, it is right for you to use that gift, unless the unction of the Spirit is upon you. Unless you adhere to this word, every assembly where you are will be broken up, and you will cause trouble. Until you come to a right understanding of the Scriptures, you will never be pleasing to God.

You have to be very careful that you never use tongues and interpretation in confusion with prophecy. When prophecy is going forth and the truth is being heard and all the people are receiving it with joy and are being built up, then there is no room for tongues or interpretation. But just at the time when the language in my heart seems too big to express, then tongues come forth and God looses the whole thing, and we get a new purpose in that.

So, you who have this wonderful gift of tongues must see to it that you never break in where the Spirit is having perfect rightofway. But when the Spirit is working with you, and you know there is a line of truth that the Lord desires to express, then let the name of God be glorified.

You see, God wants everything to be in perfect order by the Spirit. That is why Paul said, *"If any man speak in an unknown tongue, let it be by two, or at the most by three"* (1 Corinthians 14:27). You will never find me speaking if three have spoken before me, and you will never find me interpreting any word in tongues if three have spoken already. This is in order to keep the bonds of peace in the body so that the people will not be weary, because there are some people who have known nothing about what is right.

Unless you come to the Word of God, you will be in confusion and you will be in judgment. God does not want you to be in confusion or in judgment, but He wants you to be built up by the Scriptures, for the Scriptures are clear.

If the Lord reveals truth to me, and if I have said anything previously in relation to this that has not been absolutely scriptural, I will no longer say it. I allow God's Word to be my judge. If I find that anything I have said is not scriptural, I repent before God. As God is my judge, I never say anything unless I believe it is the sincere truth, but if I find out later that it is not exactly in the most perfect keeping with the Word of God, I never say it again.

Thought for today: May the Lord help us to be true to God first; then, if we are true to God, we will be true to ourselves.

DAY 73

PEACE AND HOPE

Now may the God of hope fill you with all joy and peace in believing, that you may abound in hope by the power of the Holy Spirit.
—Romans 15:13 NKJV

Scripture reading: Ephesians 1:2–21

Through sanctification of the Spirit, you will come to a place of rest. There is a peace in sanctification because it is a place of revelation, taking you into heavenly realms. God comes, speaks, and makes Himself known to you, and when you are face-to-face with God, you receive a peace "*which passes all understanding*" (Philippians 4:7), lifting you to a state of inexpressible wonderment.

Oh, this is like heaven to me,
This is like heaven to me,
I've crossed over Jordan to Canaan's fair land;
And this is like heaven to me.

This sanctification of the Spirit brings us into definite alignment with the wonderful hope of the glory of God. Lively hope is movement. It presses forward. Lively hope leaves everything behind. It keeps the vision. Lively hope sees Him coming! And you live in it—this lively hope. You are not trying to make yourself feel that you are believing, but the lively hope fills you with joy and expectation of the King's coming. Praise the Lord! I want you to know that God has this experience in His mind for you.

I pray God the Holy Spirit that He will move you this way. I trust that you will be so reconciled to God that there is not one thing that would interfere with your possessing this lively hope.

How He loves us, hovers over us, rejoices in us! How the Lord by the Holy Spirit fills our cup full and running over! (See Psalm 23:5.) "*The joy of the LORD is your strength*" (Nehemiah 8:10). I hope you won't forget the lively hope. It is the purpose of God for your soul. It is wonderful. Hallelujah!

Thought for today: A lively hope is the opposite of a dead hope.

DAY 74

REJOICE IN BEING PURIFIED

That the trial of your faith, being much more precious than of gold that perishes, though it be tried with fire, might be found to praise and honor and glory at the appearing of Jesus Christ.
—1 Peter 1:7

Scripture reading: 2 Corinthians 4:7–5:9

You have no idea what God will mean to you in trials and temptations—it is purification of the Spirit. Gold perishes, but faith never perishes; it is more precious than gold, though it may be tried with fire. I went into a place one day, and a gentleman said to me, "Would you like to see purification of gold this morning?" I replied, "Yes." He got some gold and put it in a crucible and put a blast of heat on it. First, it became bloodred, and then it changed and changed. Then this man took an instrument and passed it over the gold, drawing something off that was foreign to the gold. He did this several times until every part was taken away. "Look," he said, and there we both saw our faces in the gold. It was wonderful.

Dear believer, the trial of your faith is much more precious than gold that perishes. When God purifies you through trials, misunderstandings, persecution, and suffering because you are wrongfully judged, Jesus has given you the keynote: rejoice in that day. He is cleaning away all the dross from your life, and every evil power, until He sees His face right in your life.

"Always bearing about in the body the dying of the Lord Jesus, that the life also of Jesus might be made manifest in our body" (2 Corinthians 4:10). This process may not seem to any of us to be very joyous because it is not acceptable to the flesh, but I have told you already that your flesh is against the Spirit. Your flesh and all your human powers have to be perfectly submitted

to the mighty power of God inwardly, to express and manifest His glory outwardly. You must be willing for the process and say "Amen" to God. It may be very hard, but God will help you.

It is lovely to know that in the chastening times, in the times of misunderstanding and hard tests when you are in the right and are treated as though you were in the wrong, God is meeting you and blessing you. People say it is the devil. Never mind, let the fire burn; it will do you good. Don't begin complaining, but endure the situation joyfully. It is so sweet to understand that *"love suffers long and is kind"* (1 Corinthians 13:4 NKJV). How lovely to get to a place where you think no evil, you are not easily provoked, and you can bear all things and endure all things! Praise the Lord. Oh, the glory of it, the joy of it!

I understand what it means to jump for joy. I could jump for joy because of the Lord.

I know the Lord, I know the Lord,
I know the Lord has laid His hand on me.

"Whom having not seen, you love; in whom, though now you see Him not, yet believing, you rejoice with joy unspeakable and full of glory" (1 Peter 1:8). We love our Lord Jesus Christ, whom we have not seen. There is no voice so gentle, so soft, so full of tenderness to me. There is no voice like His, and there is no touch like His. Is it possible to love the One we have not seen? God will make it possible to all. *"Though now you see Him not, yet believing, you rejoice with joy unspeakable and full of glory."*

Thought for today: Beloved, as you are tested in the fire, the Master is purifying everything that cannot bring out His image in you.

DAY 75

SPIRITUAL DRUNKENNESS

For whether we be beside ourselves, it is to God: or whether we be sober, it is for your cause.
—2 Corinthians 5:13

Scripture reading: Psalm 96

There is a place to reach in the Holy Spirit that is mystifying to the world and to many people who are not going on with God. Here is a most remarkable lesson. We can be so filled with the Spirit, so clothed upon by Him, so purified within, so made ready for the rapture, that all the time it is as if we are drunk.

When I come in contact with people who would criticize my drunkenness, I am sober. I can be sober one minute; I can be drunk in the Spirit the next. I tell you, to be drunk with the presence of God is wonderful! *"And be not drunk with wine, wherein is excess; but be filled with the Spirit"* (Ephesians 5:18). In this there is a lively hope, filled with unconcern in regard to what anyone else thinks.

Consider a man who is drunk. He stops at a lamppost, and he has a lot to say to it. He says the most foolish things possible, and the people say, "He's lost his senses."

Oh, Lord, that I may be so drunk with You that it makes no difference what people think! I am speaking to the Lord in hymns and spiritual songs, making my boast in the Lord. The Lord of Hosts is around me, and I am so free in the Holy Spirit that I am ready to be taken to heaven. But He does not take me. Why not? I am ready, and it is better for me to go, but for the church's sake it is preferable that I stay. (See Philippians 1:23–25.)

It is best that I am clothed with the Spirit, living in the midst of the people, showing no nakedness. I need to be full of purity, full of power, full of revelation for the church's sake. It is far better to go to heaven now, but for the church's sake, I must stay, so that I may be helpful, telling others how they can have their nakedness covered, how their minds can be clothed, how all their inward impurities can be made pure in the presence of God. It is better that I am living, walking, and acting in the Holy Spirit. This may seem impossible, yet this is the height that God wants us to reach.

Here is another verse to help you: *"And if Christ be in you, the body is dead because of sin; but the Spirit is life because of righteousness"* (Romans 8:10). There is no such thing as having liberty in your body if there is any sin there. When righteousness is there, righteousness abounds. When Christ is in your heart, enthroning your life, and sin is dethroned, then righteousness abounds and the Holy Spirit has great liberty.

"And if children, then heirs; heirs of God, and joint-heirs with Christ" (v. 17). My, what triumphs of height, of length, of depth, and of breadth there are in this holy place! Where is it? Right inside. Freedom, purity, power, and separateness are ours, and we are ready for the great trumpet!

Thought for today: Holiness is the habitation of God.

DAY 76

THE RICHES OF HIS GLORY

The very God of peace sanctify you wholly.
—1 Thessalonians 5:23

Scripture reading: 1 Thessalonians 5:8–24

May the Lord of Hosts so surround us with revelation and blessing that our bodies get to the place where they can scarcely contain the joys of the Lord. He will bring us to so rich a place that forever we will know we are only the Lord's. What a blessed state of grace to be brought into, where we know that the body, the soul, and the spirit are preserved blameless until the coming of the Lord! (See 1 Thessalonians 5:23.)

God is greatly desirous for us to have more of His presence. We have only one purpose in mind: to strengthen you, to build you up in the most holy faith, and to present you for every good work so that you should be faultless in Him, quickened by the might of the Spirit, so that you might be prepared for everything that God has for you in the future. Our human nature may be brought to a place where it is so superabundantly attended to by God so that in the body we will know nothing but the Lord of Hosts.

To this end, I invite you to the banquet that cannot be exhausted, a supply beyond all human thought, an abundance beyond all human extravagances.

Are you ready to be brought by the power of God into His new plan of righteousness? Are you ready to be able as never before to leave the things of the world behind and press on toward the prize of the high calling? (See Philippians 3:13–14.)

Are you ready to be so in God's plan that you will feel God's hand upon you? You will know that He has chosen you, so that you might be a firstfruit unto God.

Are you ready for the Lord to have His choice, so that His will and purpose will be yours, so that the "Amen" of His character may sweep through your very nature, and so that you may know as you have never known before that this is the day of the visitation between you and Him?

Thought for today: No matter how you come into great faith and believing in God, God says, "Much more abundantly, much more."

DAY 77

EXPERIENCE HIS JOY

Count it all joy when you fall into divers temptations.
—James 1:2

Scripture reading: James 1:2–18

Perhaps you have been counting it all sadness when trials come. Never mind. Tell it to Jesus now. Express your deepest feelings to Him:

He knows it all, He knows it all,
My Father knows, He knows it all,
The bitter tears, how fast they fall,
He knows, my Father knows it all.

Sorrow may come at night, but *"joy comes in the morning"* (Psalm 30:5). So many believers never look up. When Jesus raised Lazarus from the dead, He lifted His eyes and said, *"Father, I thank You that You have heard Me"* (John 11:41). God wants us to have a resurrection touch about us. Never use your human plan when God speaks His Word. You have your cue from an almighty source whose resources never fade away. His treasury is past measuring, abounding with extravagances of abundance, waiting to be poured out upon us.

Hear what the Scripture says: *"God...gives to all men liberally, and upbraids not"* (James 1:5). The almighty hand of God comes to our weakness and says, "If you will dare to trust Me and not doubt, I will abundantly satisfy you from the treasure house of the Most High." He forgives, He supplies, He opens the door into His fullness and makes us know that He has done it all. When you come to Him, He gives you an overflow without measure, an expression of a Father's love.

He can satisfy every need. He satisfies the hungry with good things. (See Luke 1:53.) Will you cast *"all your care upon Him; for He cares for you"* (1 Peter 5:7)? God will help us. Glory to God. How He meets the needs of the hungry!

Thought for today: We may enter into things that will bring us sorrow and trouble, but through them, God will bring us to a deeper knowledge of Himself.

DAY 78

TRUE WORSHIP

God is a Spirit: and they that worship Him must worship Him in spirit and in truth.
—John 4:24

Scripture reading: John 4:1–30

We appreciate cathedrals and churches, but God does not dwell in temples made by hands but in the sanctuary of the heart. (See Acts 7:48.) The Father seeks *"true worshippers"* who will worship Him *"in spirit and truth"* (John 4:23). The church is the body of Christ. Its worship is a heart worship, a longing to come into the presence of God. God sees our hearts and will open our understanding. The Lord delights in His people. He wants us to come to a place of undisturbed rest and peace that is found only in God. Only simplicity will bring us there.

As Jesus placed a little child in the middle of the disciples, He said, *"Except you be converted, and become as little children, you shall not enter into the kingdom of heaven"* (Matthew 18:3). He did not mean that we should seek to have a child's mind, but a child's meek and gentle spirit. It is the only place to meet God. He will give us that place of worship.

How my heart cries out for a living faith and a deep vision of God. The world cannot produce it. It is a place where we see the Lord, a place where we pray and know that God hears. We can ask God and believe Him for the answer, having no fear but a living faith to come into the presence of God. *"In Your presence is fullness of joy; at Your right hand there are pleasures for evermore"* (Psalm 16:11).

Thought for today: Everyone who is born of God is kept alive by a power that he cannot see but can feel, a power that is generated in glory, comes down into earthen vessels, and returns to the throne of God.

DAY 79

CHANGED BY GOD

Let us not love in word, neither in tongue; but in deed and in truth.
—1 John 3:18

Scripture reading: 1 John 3:1–17

God is looking for people in whom He can reveal Himself. I used to have a tremendous temper, going white with passion. My whole nature was outside of God in that way. God knew I could never be of service to the world unless I was wholly sanctified. I was difficult to please. My wife was a good cook, but I could always find something wrong with the meal. I heard her testify in a meeting that after God sanctified me, I was pleased with everything she served.

I had men working for me, and I wanted to be a good testimony to them. One day, they waited after work was over and said, "We would like that spirit you have." There is a place of death and life where Christ reigns in the body. Then all is well. This Word is full of stimulation. It is by faith that we come into a place of grace. Then all can see that we have been made new. The Holy Spirit arouses our attention. He has something special to say: if you will believe, you can be sons of God, like Him in character, spirit, longings, and actions until all know that you are His child.

The Spirit of God can change our nature. God is the Creator. His Word is creative, and if you believe, His creative power can change your whole nature. You can become *"sons of God"* (John 1:12). You cannot reach this altitude of faith alone. No man can keep himself. The all-powerful God spreads His covering over you, saying, *"If you can believe, all things are possible to him that believes"* (Mark 9:23). The old nature is so difficult to manage. You have been ashamed of it many times, but the Lord Himself offers the answer. He says, "Come, and I will give you peace and strength.

I will change you. I will operate on you by My power, making you a '*new creature*' (2 Corinthians 5:17) if you will believe."

Jesus says, "*Learn of Me; for I am meek and lowly in heart: and you shall find rest to your souls*" (Matthew 11:29). The world has no rest. It is full of troubles, but in Christ, you can move and act in the power of God with a peace that "*passes all understanding*" (Philippians 4:7). An inward flow of divine power will change your nature. "*Therefore the world knows us not, because it knew Him not*" (1 John 3:1).

What does this mean? I have lived in one house for fifty years. I have preached from my own doorstep; all around, people know me. They know me when they need someone to pray, when there is trouble, when they need a word of wisdom. But at Christmastime when they call their friends to celebrate, would they invite me? No. Why? They would say, "He is sure to want a prayer meeting, but we want a party."

Wherever Jesus came, sin was revealed, and men don't like sin to be revealed. Sin separates us from God forever. You are in a good place when you weep before God, repenting over the least thing. If you have spoken unkindly, you realized it was not like the Lord. Your keen conscience has taken you to prayer. It is a wonderful thing to have a sensitive conscience. When everything is wrong, you cry to the Lord. It is when we are close to God that our hearts are revealed. God intends for us to live in purity, seeing Him all the time.

Thought for today: Our human spirit has to be controlled by the Holy Spirit.

DAY 80

EQUIPPED FOR SERVICE

Blessed are they which are persecuted for righteousness' sake: for theirs is the kingdom of heaven.
—Matthew 5:10

Scripture reading: Romans 12:1–13

We can be equipped with the power of God. I want you to keep your minds fixed on this fact, for it will help to establish you. It will strengthen you if you think about Paul, who was *"one born out of due time"* (1 Corinthians 15:8).

Paul was *"a brand plucked out of the fire"* (Zechariah 3:2), chosen by God to be an apostle to the Gentiles. (See Ephesians 3:1.) I want you to see him, first as a persecutor, furious to destroy those who were bringing glad tidings to the people. See how madly he rushed them into prison, urging them to blaspheme the holy name of Christ. Then see this man changed by the power of Christ and the gospel of God. See him divinely transformed by God, filled with the Holy Spirit. As you read the ninth chapter of Acts, you see how special his calling was. In order for Paul to understand how he might be able to minister to the needy, God's Son said to Ananias, *"I will show him how great things he must suffer for My name's sake"* (Acts 9:16).

I don't want you to think I mean suffering with diseases. I mean suffering in persecution, with slander, strife, bitterness, abusive scoldings, and with many other evil ways of suffering; but none of these things will hurt you. Instead, they will kindle a fire of holy ambition within you.

To be persecuted for Christ's sake is to be united with a blessed people, with those chosen to cry under the altar, *"How long?"* (Revelation 6:10). Oh, to know that we may cooperate with Jesus. If we suffer persecution, rejoice in that day. Beloved, God wants witnesses, witnesses of truth, witnesses to the full truth, witnesses to the fullness of redemption, witnesses to the deliverance from the power of sin and disease, witnesses who can claim their territory, because of the eternal power working in them, eternal life beautifully, gloriously filling the body, until the body is filled with the life of the Spirit. God wants us to believe that we may be ministers of that kind.

Paul was lost in the zeal of his ministry. Those first disciples gathered together on the first day of the week to break bread. (See Acts 20:7.) See their need for breaking bread. As they were gathered together, they were caught up with the ministry. In Switzerland, the people said to me, "How long can you preach to us?" I said, "When the Holy Spirit is upon me, I can preach forever!"

If it were only man's ability or college training, we might be crazy before we began, but if it is the Holy Spirit's ministry, we will be as sound as a bell that has no flaw in it. It will be the Holy Spirit at the first, in the middle, and at the end. I do not want to think of anything during the preaching so that the preaching will reflect nothing except, "Thus says the Lord." The preaching of Jesus is that blessed incarnation, that glorious freedom from bondage, that blessed power that liberates from sin and the powers of darkness, that glorious salvation that saves you from death to life, and from the power of Satan to God.

Thought for today: The cup of suffering from heaven is united with a baptism of fire.

DAY 81

THE NEED FOR HUMILITY

Serving the Lord with all humility.
—Acts 20:19

Scripture reading: James 4

None of us will be able to be ministers of the new covenant of promise in the power of the Holy Spirit without humility. It is clear to me that in the measure that the death of the Lord is in me, the life of the Lord will abound in me. To me, the baptism of the Holy Spirit is not a goal; it is an infilling that allows us to reach the highest level, the holiest position that it is possible for human nature to reach. The baptism of the Holy Spirit comes to reveal Him who is filled fully with God.

To be baptized with the Holy Spirit is to be baptized into death, into life, into power, into fellowship with the Trinity, where we cease to be and God takes us forever. Paul said, *"I am crucified with Christ: nevertheless I live; yet not I, but Christ lives in me"* (Galatians 2:20). I believe that God wants to put His hand upon us so that we may reach ideal definitions of humility, of human helplessness, of human insufficiency, until we will rest no more upon human plans but have God's thoughts, God's voice, and God the Holy Spirit to speak to us. Now here is a word for us: *"And now, behold, I go bound in the Spirit"* (Acts 20:22). There is the Word. Is that a possibility? Is there a possibility for a person to align himself so completely with the divine will of God?

Jesus was a man, flesh and blood like us, while at the same time, He was the incarnation of divine authority, power, and majesty of the glory of heaven. He bore in His body the weaknesses of human flesh. He was tempted *"in all points...as we are, yet without sin"* (Hebrews 4:15). He is so lovely, such a perfect Savior. Oh, that I could shout "Jesus" in such a way that the world would hear. There is salvation, life, power, and deliverance through His name. But, beloved, I see that "*the Spirit drives Him*" (Mark 1:12), that He was "*led by the Spirit*" (Luke 4:1), and here comes Paul "*bound in the Spirit*" (Acts 20:22).

What an ideal condescension of heaven that God should lay hold of humanity and possess it with His holiness, His righteousness, His truth, and His faith so that Paul could say, "'*I go bound*' (v. 22); I have no choice. The only choice is for God. The only desire or ambition is God's. I am bound with God." Is it possible, beloved?

If you look at the first chapter of Galatians, you will see how wonderfully Paul rose to this state of bliss. If you look at the third chapter of Ephesians, you see how he became "*less than the least of all saints*" (v. 8). In Acts 26, you will hear him say, "*King Agrippa, I was not disobedient to the heavenly vision*" (v. 19). In order to keep the vision, he yielded not to flesh and blood. God laid hold of him; God bound him; God preserved him. I ought to say, however, that it is a wonderful position to be preserved by the Almighty. We ought to see to it in our Christian experience that when we commit ourselves to God, the consequences will be all right. "*Whosoever shall seek to save his life shall lose it; and whosoever shall lose his life shall preserve it*" (Luke 17:33).

What is it to be bound by the Almighty, preserved by the Infinite? There is no end to God's resources. They reach right into glory. They never finish on the earth. God takes control of a man in the baptism of the Holy Spirit as he yields himself to God. There is the possibility of being taken and yet left—taken charge of by God and left in the world to carry out His commands. That is one of God's possibilities for humanity: to be taken over by the power of God while being left in the world to be salt as the Scripture describes. (See Matthew 5:13.)

Thought for today: The way to get up is to get down.

DAY 82

A FRESH VISION FOR EACH DAY

His compassions fail not. They are new every morning.
—Lamentations 3:22–23

Scripture reading: Psalm 62

I am out to win souls. It is my business to seek the lost. It is my business to make everybody hungry, dissatisfied, mad, or glad. I want to see every person filled with the Holy Spirit. I must have a message from heaven that will not leave people as I found them. Something must happen if we are filled with the Holy Spirit. Something must happen at every place. Men must know that a man filled with the Holy Spirit is no longer a man. A man can be swept by the power of God in his first stage of revelation of Christ, and from that moment on, he has to be an extraordinary man. In order to be filled with the Holy Spirit, he has to become a free body for God to dwell in.

I appeal to you who have been filled with the Holy Spirit: whatever the cost, let God have His way. I appeal to you who have to move on, who cannot rest until God does something for you. God has been revealing to me that anyone who does not sin yet remains in the same place spiritually for a week is a backslider. You say, "How is it possible?" Because God's revelation is available to anyone who will wholeheartedly be committed to following God.

Staying the same for two days would almost indicate that you had lost the vision. The child of God must have a fresh vision every day. The child of God must be more active by the Holy Spirit every day. The child of God must come into line with the power of heaven, where he knows that God has put His hand upon him.

Jesus went about doing good, for God was with Him. God anointed Him. Beloved, is that not the ministry to which God would have us become heirs? Why? Because the Holy Spirit has to bring us a revelation of Jesus, and the purpose of being filled with the Holy Spirit is to give us a revelation of Jesus. He will make the Word of God just the same life as was given by the Son, as new, as fresh, as effective as if the Lord Himself were speaking.

I wonder how many of you are a part of the bride of Christ? The bride loves to hear the Bridegroom's voice. (See John 3:29.) Here it is, the blessed Word of God, the whole Word, not just part of it. No, we believe in the whole thing. Day by day, we find out that the Word itself gives life. The Spirit of the Lord breathes through us. He makes the Word come alive in our hearts and minds. So, I have within my hands, within my heart, within my mind, this blessed reservoir of promises that is able to do so many marvelous things.

God has indeed been manifesting Himself. I must tell you one of those cases. In Oakland, California, I held meetings at a theater. Only to glorify God, I tell you that Oakland was in a very serious state. There was very little Pentecostal work there, and so a large theater was rented. God worked especially in filling the place until we had to have overflow meetings. In these meetings, we had a rising flood of people getting saved by standing up voluntarily, all over that place, getting saved the moment they stood. Then we had a large number of people who needed help in their bodies, rising up in faith and being healed.

One of them was an old man who was ninety-five years of age. He had been suffering for three years until he gradually got to the place that for three weeks he was consuming only liquids. He was in a terrible state, but this man was different from the others. I got him to stand while I prayed for him, and he came back and told us with such a radiant face that new life had come into his body. He said, "I am ninety-five years old. When I came into the meeting, I was full of pain with cancer in the stomach. I have been healed so that I have been eating perfectly, and I have no pain." Similarly, many people were healed.

I hope you are expecting big things.

Thought for today: No man can have the Trinity abiding in him and be the same as he was before.

DAY 83

UNITY OF THE SPIRIT

Endeavoring to keep the unity of the Spirit in the bond of peace.
—Ephesians 4:3

Scripture reading: Psalm 133

You are bound forever out of loyalty to God to see that no division comes into the church body, to see that nothing comes into the assembly, as it came into David's flock, to tear and rend the body. You have to be careful. If a person comes along with a prophecy and you find that it is tearing down and bringing trouble, denounce it accordingly; judge it by the Word. You will find that all true prophecy will be perfectly full of hopefulness. It will have compassion; it will have comfort; it will have edification. So, if anything comes into the church that you know is hurting the flock and disturbing the assembly, you must see to it that you begin to pray so that this thing is put to death.

Bring unity in the bonds of perfection so that the church of God will receive edification. Then the church will begin to be built up in the faith and the establishing of truth, and believers will be one. There is one body. Recognize that fact. When schism comes into the body, believers always act as though there were more than one body.

Do not forget that God means for us to be very faithful to the church so that we do not allow anything to come into the church to break up the body. You cannot find anything in the body in its relation to Christ that has schism in it. Christ's life in the body—there is no schism in that. When Christ's life comes into the church, there will be no discord; there will be a perfect blending of heart and hand, and it will be lovely. Endeavor *"to keep the unity of the Spirit in the bond of peace."*

Thought for today: When we think that the church is poor and needy, we forget that the spirit of intercession can unlock every safe in the world.

DAY 84

THE FLOOD TIDE OF REVIVAL

Will You not revive us again: that Your people may rejoice in You?
—Psalm 85:6

Scripture reading: Psalm 85:7–86:13

Wherever Jesus went, multitudes followed Him, because He lived, moved, breathed, was swallowed up, clothed, and filled by God. He was God; and as the Son of Man, the Spirit of God—the Spirit of creative holiness—rested upon Him. It is lovely to be holy. Jesus came to impart to us the Spirit of holiness.

We are only at the edge of things; the almighty plan for the future is marvelous. God must do something to increase. We need a revival to revive all we touch within us and outside of us. We need a flood tide with a deluge behind it. Jesus left 120 men to turn the world upside down. (See Acts 1:15.) The Spirit is upon us to change our situation. We must move on; we must let God increase in us for the deliverance of multitudes; and we must travail until souls are born and quickened into a new relationship with heaven. Jesus had divine authority with power, and He left it for us. We must preach truth, holiness, and purity "*in the inward parts*" (Psalm 51:6). Thirst for more of God.

Jesus treaded the winepress alone (see Isaiah 63:3), despising the cross and the shame. He bore it all alone so that we might be "*partakers of the divine nature*" (2 Peter 1:4), sharers in the divine plan of holiness. That's revival—Jesus manifesting divine authority. He was without sin. People saw the Lamb of God in a new way. Hallelujah! Let us live in holiness, and revival will come down, and God will enable us to do the work to which we are appointed. All Jesus said came to pass: signs, wonders, mighty deeds. Only believe, and yield, and yield, until all the vision is fulfilled.

Thought for today: Jesus was not only holy, but He also loved holiness.

DAY 85

THE SPIRIT IS UPON ME

The Spirit of the Lord is upon Me.
—Luke 4:18

Scripture reading: Luke 4:1–21

I believe God is bringing us to a place where we know that the Spirit of the Lord is upon us. If we have not gotten to that place, God wants to bring us to the fact of what Jesus said in John 14: *"I will pray the Father, and He shall give you another Comforter, that He may abide with you for ever"* (v. 16). Because the Spirit of the Lord came upon Him who is our Head, we must see to it that we receive the same anointing, and that the same Spirit is upon us. The devil will cause us to lose the victory if we allow ourselves to be defeated by him. But it is a fact that the Spirit of the Lord is upon us, and as for me, I have no message apart from the message He will give, and I believe that the signs He speaks of will follow.

I believe that Jesus was the One sent forth from God and the propitiation for the sins of the whole world. (See 1 John 2:2.) We see the manifestation of the Spirit resting upon Him so that His ministry was with power. May God awaken us to the fact that this is the only place where there is any ministry of power.

The Comforter has come. He has come, and He has come to abide forever. Are you going to be defeated by the devil? No, for the Comforter has come so that we may receive and give forth the signs that must follow, so that we may not by any means be deceived by the schemes of the devil. There is no limit to what we may become if we dwell and live in the Spirit. In the Spirit of prayer, we are taken right away from earth into heaven. In the Spirit, the Word of God seems to unfold in a wonderful way, and it is only in the Spirit that the love of God is poured out in us. (See Romans 5:5.)

Thought for today: Who is the man who is willing to lay down everything so that he may have God's all?

DAY 86

THE PROPER USE OF LIBERTY

Where the Spirit of the Lord is, there is liberty.
—2 Corinthians 3:17

Scripture reading: Galatians 5:1–15

We must never abuse liberty; we must be in the place where liberty can use us. If we misuse liberty, we will be as dead as possible, and our efforts will all end with a fizzle. But if we are in the Spirit, the Lord of Life is the same Spirit. I believe it is right to jump for joy, but don't jump until the joy makes you jump, because if you do, you will jump flat. If you jump as the joy makes you jump, you will bounce up again.

In the Spirit, there is a divine plan. If Pentecostal people come into this plan in meekness and in the true knowledge of God, every heart in each meeting will be moved by the Spirit.

Liberty has many aspects to it, but no liberty is going to help people as much as testimony. I find people who don't know how to testify properly. We must testify only as the Spirit gives utterance. We find in the book of Revelation that *"the testimony of Jesus is the spirit of prophecy"* (Revelation 19:10).

Sometimes our flesh keeps us down, but our hearts are so full that they lift us up. Have you ever been like that? The flesh is fastening you to your seat, but your heart is bubbling over. At last the heart has more power, and you stand up. Then, in that heart affection for Jesus, in the Spirit of love and in the knowledge of truth, you begin to testify, and when you are done, you sit down. Liberty used wrongly goes on after you have finished saying what God wants you to say, and it spoils the meeting. Do not use your liberty except for the glory of God.

So many churches are spoiled by long prayers and long testimonies. If he stays in the Spirit, the speaker can tell when he should sit down. When you begin to speak your own words, people get tired and wish that you would sit down. The anointing ceases, and you sit down worse than when you rose up.

It is nice for a person to begin cold and warm up as he goes on. When he catches fire and sits down in the midst of it, he will keep the fire afterward. Look! It is lovely to pray, and it is a joy to hear you pray, but when you go on and on after you are truly done, all the people get tired of it.

This excellent glory should go on to a liberality to everybody, and this would prove that all the church is in liberty. The church ought to be free so that the people always go away feeling, "Oh, I wish the meeting had gone on for another hour!" or "What a glorious time we had at that prayer meeting!" or "Wasn't that testimony meeting a revelation!" That is the way to finish up. Never finish up with something too long; finish up with something too short. Then everybody comes again eager to pick up where they left off.

Thought for today: We are not to use liberty because we have it to use, but we are to let the liberty use us.

DAY 87

THE BEST IS YET TO COME

Forgetting those things which are behind, and reaching forth to those things which are before, I press toward the mark for the prize of the high calling of God in Christ Jesus.
—Philippians 3:13–14

Scripture reading: Colossians 1:9–18

When Jesus was thirty years old, the time came when it was made manifest at the Jordan River that He was the Son of God. How beautifully it was made known! It had to be made known first to one who was full of the vision of God. The vision comes to those who are full of God. When God has you in His own plan, what a change; how things operate! You see things in a new light. God is being greatly glorified as you yield from day to day. The Spirit seems to lay hold of you and bring you further along. Yes, it is a pressing on, and then He gives us touches of His wonderful power, manifestations of the glory, and indications of greater things to follow. These days that we are living in now speak of even better days to come.

Where would we be today if we had stopped short, if we had not fulfilled the vision that God gave us? I am thinking about the time when Christ sent the Spirit. Saul, who later became the apostle Paul, did not know much about the Spirit. His heart was stirred against the followers of Jesus, his eyes were blinded to the truth, and he was going to put the newborn church to an end in a short time; but Jesus was looking on. We can scarcely understand the whole process—only as God seems to show us—when He gets us into His plan and works with us little by little.

We are all amazed that we are among the "tongues people." Some of us would never have been in this Pentecostal movement if we had not been drawn, but God has a wonderful way of drawing us. Paul never intended to be among the disciples; he never intended to have anything to do with this Man called Jesus. But God was working. In the same way, God has been working with us and has brought us to this place. It is marvelous! Oh, the vision of God, the wonderful manifestation that God has for Israel!

I have one purpose in my heart, and it is surely God's plan for me: I want you to see that Jesus Christ is the greatest manifestation in all the world, and that His power is unequaled, but that there is only one way to minister it. Some of the people in Ephesus, after they had seen Paul working wonders by the power of Christ, began to act in human ways. (See Acts 19.) If I want to do anything for God, I see that it is necessary for me to get the knowledge of God. I cannot work on my own; I must get the vision of God. It must be a divine revelation of the Son of God. It must be that.

I can see as clearly as anything that Saul, in his mad pursuit, had to be stopped along the way. After he was stopped and had the vision from heaven and the light from heaven, he instantly realized that he had been working in the wrong way. As soon as the power of the Holy Spirit fell upon him, he began in the way in which God wanted him to go, and it was wonderful how he had to suffer to come into that way. (See Acts 9:15–16.) A broken spirit, a tried life, and being driven into a corner as if some strange thing had happened (see 1 Peter 4:12)—these are surely the ways in which we to get to know the way of God.

Thought for today: Did it ever strike you that we cannot be too full for a vision, that we cannot have too much of God?

DAY 88

LET KINGDOM LIFE REIGN

Let every one of us please his neighbor for his good to edification.
—Romans 15:2

Scripture reading: Romans 14:12–15:2

If it is only a finger or a tooth that aches, if it is only a corn on your foot that pinches you or anything in the body that detracts from the highest spiritual attainment, the kingdom of heaven is dethroned to a degree; *"the kingdom of heaven suffers violence"* (Matthew 11:12).

By the Word of God, I am proving to you that the kingdom of heaven is within you. *"Greater is He that is in you"* (1 John 4:4)—the Son of God, the kingdom of heaven within you—*"than he that is in the world"* (v. 4)—the power of Satan outside you.

Disease or weakness, or any distraction in you, is a power of violence that can take the kingdom of heaven in you by force. The same spiritual power that will reveal this to you will relieve you. On the authority of the Word of God, I maintain that *"greater is He that is in you"* (v. 4) than any power of Satan that is around you. How much more would be done if you would inwardly claim your rights and deliver yourselves!

I believe the Bible from front to back. If, by the power of God, I put in you an audacity, a determination, so that you won't let Satan rest, you will be victorious. Praise the Lord!

Why do I take this attitude? Because for every step of my life since my baptism, I have had to pay the price of everything for others. God has to take me through to the place so that I may be able to show the people how to do it. Some people come up to me and say, "I have been waiting for the baptism, and I am having such a struggle. I am having to fight for every inch of it. Isn't it strange?" No. A thousand to one, God is preparing you to help somebody else who is desiring to receive it.

The reason I am so firm about the necessity of getting the baptism in the Holy Spirit, and about the significance of the Spirit's making a manifestation when He comes in, is this: I fought it. I went to a meeting because I had heard people were speaking in tongues there. I forced myself on the attention of those in the meeting almost like a man who was mad. I told the people there, "This meeting of yours is nothing. I have left better conditions at home. I am hungry and thirsty for something."

"What do you want?" they asked.
"I want tongues."
"You want the baptism?" they asked.
"Not I," I said. "I have the baptism. I want tongues."

I could have had a fight with anybody. The whole situation was this: God was training me for something else. The power of God fell upon my body with such ecstasy of joy that I could not satisfy the joy within with my natural tongue; then I found the Spirit speaking through me in other tongues.

What did it mean? I knew that I had had anointings of joy before this, and expressions of the blessed attitude of the Spirit of Life, and joy in the Holy Spirit; I had felt it all the way through my life. But when the fullness came with a high tide, with an overflowing life, I knew that was different from anything else. And I knew that was the baptism, but God had to show me.

Thought for today: The Bible won't have an atom of power in you if you don't put it into practice in yourself.

DAY 89

UNCONDITIONAL SURRENDER

Repent you: for the kingdom of heaven is at hand.
—Matthew 3:2

Scripture reading: 2 Peter 3:1–9

Pentecost has made me rejoice in Jesus. God has been confirming His power by His Holy Spirit. I have an intense yearning to see Pentecost, and I am not seeing it. I may feel a little of the glow, but what we need is a deeper work of the Holy Spirit in order for God's message to come full of life and power and sharper than a *"twoedged sword"* (Hebrews 4:12). At Pentecost, Peter stood up in the power of the Holy Spirit, and three thousand people were saved. Not long after this, he preached again, and five thousand people were saved.

I am positive that we are on the wrong side of the cross. We talk about love, love, love, but it ought to be repent, repent, repent. John the Baptist came, and his message was *"Repent"* (Matthew 3:2). Jesus came with the same message: *"Repent"* (Matthew 4:17). The Holy Spirit came, and the message was the same: repent, repent, repent and believe. (See Acts 2:38.) What has all this to do with Pentecost? Everything! It is the secret of our failure.

Daniel carried on his heart the burden of the people. He mourned for the captivity of Zion, he confessed his sin and the people's sin, and he identified himself with Israel until God made him a flame of fire. (See Daniel 9.) The result: a remnant returned to Zion to walk in the despised way of obedience to God.

Nehemiah was brokenhearted when he learned of the desolation of Jerusalem. He pleaded for months before God, confessing his sin and the sin of his people (see Nehemiah 1), and God opened the way, and the walls and gates of the city were built up. It is the spirit of deep repentance that is needed.

Weeping is not repentance; sorrow is not repentance. Repentance is turning away from sin and doing the work of righteousness and holiness. What can we do to receive the baptism? Repent!

Thought for today: The baptism of the Holy Spirit brings a deep repentance and a demolished and impoverished spirit.

DAY 90

FULL OF LIFE

Be filled with all the fullness of God.
—Ephesians 3:19

Scripture reading: Ephesians 3:14–21

We want our whole being to be so full of the life of our Lord that the Holy Spirit can speak and act through us. We want to live always in Him. Oh, the charm of His divine plan! We cry out for the inspiration of the God of power. We want to act in the Holy Spirit. We want to breathe out divine life. We want the glory, miracles, and wonders that work out the plan of the Most High God. We want to be absorbed by God, and we want to know nothing among men except Jesus and Him crucified. (See 1 Corinthians 2:2.) Unto You, O God, be the glory and the honor and the power! (See Revelation 5:13.)

Yes, filled with God,
Yes, filled with God,
Emptied of self and filled with God.

For He is so precious to me,
For He is so precious to me;
It's heaven below
My Redeemer to know,
For He is so precious to me.

Can you wonder why I love Him so? May there be a cry until we witness Acts 11:15: *"And as I began to speak, the Holy Spirit fell upon them"* (NKJV).

Oh, be on fire, oh, be on fire,
Oh, be on fire for God.
Oh, be on fire, be all on fire,
Be all on fire for God.

Thought for today: To live two days in succession on the same spiritual plane is a tragedy.

ABOUT THE AUTHOR

An encounter with Smith Wigglesworth (1859–1947) was an unforgettable experience. This seems to be the universal reaction of all who knew him or heard him speak. Smith Wigglesworth was a simple yet remarkable man who was used in an extraordinary way by our extraordinary God. He had a contagious and inspiring faith. Under his ministry, thousands of people came to salvation, committed themselves to a deeper faith in Christ, received the baptism in the Holy Spirit, and were miraculously healed. The power that brought these kinds of results was the presence of the Holy Spirit, who filled Smith Wigglesworth and used him in bringing the good news of the gospel to people all over the world. Wigglesworth gave glory to God for everything that was accomplished through his ministry, and he wanted people to understand his work only in this context, because his sole desire was that people would see Jesus and not himself.

Smith Wigglesworth was born in England in 1859. Immediately after his conversion as a boy, he had a concern for the salvation of others and won people to Christ, including his mother. Even so, as a young man, he could not express himself well enough to give a testimony in church, much less preach a sermon. Wigglesworth said that his mother had the same difficulty in expressing herself that he did. This family trait, coupled with the fact that he had no formal education because he began working twelve hours a day at the age of seven to help support the family, contributed to Wigglesworth's awkward speaking style. He became a plumber by trade, yet he continued to devote himself to winning many people to Christ on an individual basis.

In 1882, he married Polly Featherstone, a vivacious young woman who loved God and had a gift of preaching and evangelism. It was she who taught him to read and who became his closest confidant and strongest supporter.

They both had compassion for the poor and needy in their community, and they opened a mission, at which Polly preached. Significantly, people were miraculously healed when Wigglesworth prayed for them.

In 1907, Wigglesworth's circumstances changed dramatically when, at the age of forty-eight, he was baptized in the Holy Spirit. Suddenly, he had a new power that enabled him to preach, and even his wife was amazed at the transformation. This was the beginning of what became a worldwide evangelistic and healing ministry that reached thousands. He eventually ministered in the United States, Australia, South Africa, and all over Europe. His ministry extended up to the time of his death in 1947.

Several emphases in Smith Wigglesworth's life and ministry characterize him: a genuine, deep compassion for the unsaved and sick; an unflinching belief in the Word of God; a desire that Christ should increase and he should decrease (John 3:30); a belief that he was called to exhort people to enlarge their faith and trust in God; an emphasis on the baptism in the Holy Spirit with the manifestation of the gifts of the Spirit as in the early church; and a belief in complete healing for everyone of all sickness.

Smith Wigglesworth was called "The Apostle of Faith" because absolute trust in God was a constant theme of both his life and his messages. In his meetings, he would quote passages from the Word of God and lead lively singing to help build people's faith and encourage them to act on it. He emphasized belief in the fact that God could do the impossible. He had great faith in what God could do, and God did great things through him.